AFTER SCHOOL
Communication Activity Book

HOME EXPERIENCES THAT
REINFORCE CLASSROOM LESSONS

by Anita Marcott Riley

Illustrations by Marlene Marston DeFoor

Communication Skill Builders

3830 E. Bellevue/P.O. Box 4205
Tucson, Arizona 85733
(602) 323-7500

DUPLICATING

You may prefer to copy the designated reproducible materials by using stencils or spirit masters. It is not necessary to tear pages out of this book. Make a single photocopy of the desired page. Use that photocopy to make a stencil or spirit master on a thermal copier.

ABOUT THE AUTHOR

As a teacher with the Garden City (Michigan) Public Schools' Developmental Learning Program for the Autistic, **Anita Marcott Riley** is involved with diagnosing, assessing, and programming for as many as 240 autistic and autistic-like students with cognitive and communicative abilities ranging from three months to eight years. She was awarded the M.A. degree in Speech and Language Pathology from Eastern Michigan University and the B.A. degree in General Speech and English from West Liberty State College. Ms. Riley holds the Certificate of Clinical Competence of the American Speech-Language-Hearing Association.

Also by the author and available through Communication Skill Builders:

Evaluating Acquired Skills in Communication (EASIC) (1984)
Autistic Behavior Composite Checklist and Profile (1984)

I dedicate this book to the memory of Mary Beth.

ACKNOWLEDGMENTS

I would like to express my gratitude to these people for their part in preparing this manual:

Peg Bowen
Marge Chamberlain
Debra Christian
Terry Comben
Karen Faulkner
Pat Felts
Cheryl Klobucar
Angus McMillan
Mary O'Neill
Michelle Cipriani Peters
Michael Riley
Barb Varkoly Smith
Lindsay Herbst Yoelin

Thanks also to the staff members, parents and other caregivers, and students at the Garden City (Michigan) Public Schools and Burger Developmental Learning Program for the Autistic Impaired. I appreciate their participation and cooperation in this project.

CONTENTS

INTRODUCTION

After School Communication Activity Book contains reproducible activity sheets to send home to parents and caregivers of students with autistic impairment, developmental disability, and other communication handicaps. The activity sheets provide techniques and ideas to help parents teach and reinforce skills that are being taught at school. Many of the activities incorporate functional tasks and daily routines.

Activities are presented in three achievement areas—Pre-Language, Receptive Language, and Expressive Language. The activities are based on the Communication Skills Inventories presented in *Evaluating Acquired Skills in Communication (EASIC)*. They can be coordinated with the student's Individual Education Plan (IEP) when those language inventories have been used to assess and plan the student's program.

The category and skills listed by number at the top left-hand corner of each activity sheet refer to the corresponding category and skills detailed in *EASIC*. See "Index of Skills" (pages 97-100) for cross-references between *EASIC* skills and the activity sheets in this book.

Activity sheets may be sent home weekly, biweekly, or monthly in a notebook or folder. Do not send too many sheets home at one time. Generally, parents will read, absorb, and implement suggestions from only one or two pages at a time. You may want to include your own experience stories, progress notes, or ideas for other projects that parents can do with their youngsters.

Not all activities are appropriate for each student. The student's Individual Educational Plan will provide a starting point for selecting relevant pages. Additional activity sheets should be sent home as they become appropriate to a student's developmental level and are related to the lessons being taught at school.

Parent workshops, group meetings, and individual parent conferences may be scheduled to discuss these activities and ideas. It will give parents the opportunity to ask questions, compare experiences, and discuss problems with each other and with you.

The activity sheets also may be used for inservice training for classroom teachers and paraprofessionals. Information is shared about communication techniques being used in speech classes. Those techniques then can be coordinated with classroom instruction on a regular basis.

You may need to alter some of the activity sheets to meet the individual needs of your students, to accommodate the differences in teaching styles, and to allow for different methods in carrying out the suggestions. Regardless of how you use the activity sheets, they should be presented in a practical, easy-to-use manner. They are designed to help you and your students' parents work together toward improving the students' communication skills.

We hope the activity sheets will foster a better relationship between students and parents while promoting acquisition of functional skills in daily living.

LETTER TO PARENTS

Dear Parents:

This folder contains activity sheets with suggestions for helping your student practice the same communication skills at home that we are working on at school. Some of these activities may be things you are doing already. Other activity sheets may give you some new ideas on how to improve your student's communication skills while you carry out daily routines.

We will send activity sheets to you on a regular basis. Add the new pages to this folder. It is important that your student carry the folder to school and to speech sessions so that additional pages will not get lost.

The way that we teach a skill at school may not be the same way you carry out the activity at home. By establishing a common routine, we can avoid confusing the student. We invite you to visit your student's scheduled speech sessions so you can see how we are teaching the skills. If you are planning a visit, please phone for an appointment. We will be sure to schedule activities that you are interested in, and we can avoid the disruption of having too many visitors present during any one session. Your student's speech session times are

_____

Your input is essential if this program is to be relevant and useful to you and your student. If you have any suggestions or questions, please call us at

_____

Sincerely,
The Speech Staff

Pre-Language

LEARNING BASIC SKILLS

In learning any task, several skills enhance the degree of learning that occurs.

Attending skills, the focusing of one's attention on the task at hand, are necessary for learning to communicate with others.

Eye contact also must be developed.

A person must want to communicate and have a message to convey. This is called *communicative intent.* A person also must be compliant—that is, not be resistant or negative to learning and communicating.

It is necessary to establish the skill of appropriate *physical proximity*—the distance or space between and the physical contact with others while communicating.

Social skills and *turn-taking,* the ability to be both listener and communicator, also are essential to successful communication.

The more natural it becomes for the student to use these basic skills, the easier it will be to concentrate on the other communication skills being taught. Here are some ways you can help your student develop these important communication skills.

Attending Skills
Work to establish and maintain your student's attention for short periods of time. Use lots of positive reinforcement—pats, hugs, treats, or whatever your student enjoys most—and gradually work to lengthen your student's attention span.

Eye contact
Expect eye contact when communicating.

Physical Proximity
Help your student learn how to establish appropriate physical distances and contact with others.

Social Skills and Turn-taking
Help the student learn to take turns being the listener and the communicator. Provide adequate pause time after speaking, so that the student will understand that a response is required. The need for a response can be indicated through body language—a look of expectancy, raising your eyebrows, or gesturing with a reverse wave, indicating "Come on." You may want to say "My turn" and "Your turn" while gesturing toward yourself and the student.

Communicative Intent
Determine what it is that the student is trying to communicate, help make communicating a pleasant and successful experience, and give lavish praise for all attempts.

The Speech Staff

LISTENING ACTIVITIES

Students often have difficulty responding appropriately to things they hear and see. They may need to focus attention on learning to recognize that a sound has occurred and then locating the sound source.

To develop listening skills, place a noise-making object out of your student's sight, and create the sound. A bell, a rattle, or any household items struck together may be used to make noise. At first, you may need to move the sound source away from the student's ear. Sometimes the student may not respond to a bell ringing or cymbals crashing, and other times the noise of a candy wrapper may cause a response. Practice using a variety of sounds until your student is able to locate the sound source consistently.

It is important also for students to show recognition of familiar voices and respond when their names are called. Practice name recognition with your student. Reward responses by giving lots of hugs, affection, and positive attention.

Enjoy these listening activities often, and watch your student become more aware of sounds at home and at school!

The Speech Staff

VISUAL FOCUSING, REACHING, AND GRASPING

Students frequently have difficulty focusing their attention on things they can see. At first, you may need to place an object directly in front of the student's eyes. Eventually, the student should be able to focus on the object and attend to objects that are not always placed directly ahead. Gradually move the object further away or at an angle.

When your student is able to see an object and focus on it, encourage the student to reach for and grasp it. Dangling baby toys, brightly colored objects, and desirable foods can be used to teach this skill. Vary the objects and use different places until the student can focus on, reach for, and grasp a variety of objects from a number of places. With this skill, your student will be able to explore many new objects and gain new interests.

The Speech Staff

VISUAL TRACKING ACTIVITIES

Tracking means that the student's eyes follow an object moving back and forth or up and down. The ability to track helps the student search for objects and maintain attention.

Teach your student to watch the toy car being pushed or the ball being rolled across the floor. Bounce a ball up and down to teach vertical tracking. Use a flashlight in a dark room to provide a variety of tracking directions.

At first, you may have to move the student's head. Eventually the student should be able to follow the movement while holding the head still. You also may need to limit the distances you ask the student to track. Gradually expand the tracking area by pushing the car harder, rolling the ball farther, or bouncing the ball higher.

By giving lots of these sensory stimulation exercises, you will help your student become more aware of the sights and sounds around school and at home. You also will be sharing some experiences that are fun!

The Speech Staff

UNDERSTANDING OBJECT PERMANENCE AND MEMORY

Understanding that an object exists even when it is not in sight is called *object permanence*. This skill requires the use of memory.

The length of time a student is expected to remember an object after it has been hidden may be only a few seconds at first. The eventual goal is for the student to remember over longer and longer periods of time.

Show your student a favorite small toy or food. Then, making sure the student is watching, hide the item under a paper towel or washcloth. Help the student find the hidden item. Allow the student to eat the food or play with the toy for a few minutes. If the student has difficulty finding the toy or food, try again; but this time, only partially cover the object. Gradually cover more of it as the student becomes more successful. Eventually, cover the whole item.

To develop a longer attention span and memory, require the student to wait for longer periods of time before being allowed to find the object.

Once the student can find the object under one cover, increase the number of covers to two and eventually three. Small food items can be hidden in the mouth of a puppet, and toys can be placed under a variety of small containers. Any number of household items can be used as covers, and any small desirable object may be chosen as the hidden treasure.

Students really enjoy these activities! Help your student improve memory and understanding of object permanence by going on these "treasure hunts."

The Speech Staff

FUNCTIONS OF OBJECTS AND CAUSALITY

Learning to use objects from the environment is an important skill that benefits students in their daily living activities. It is a skill that has many levels. The simplest level is to be able to use an object that requires only one step. For example, using a tissue requires only the motion of wiping the nose. Other objects that have simple functions include:

cup	spoon	light switch
hat	door	chair

Some objects that have more complex functions are:

shoes	sink and faucets
toothbrush and toothpaste	drinking fountain
soap and washcloth	mechanical toys
comb and brush	crayons and paper

Use the "Can Do" Chart to list the objects your student uses independently. Then think of other objects that your student must learn how to use in order to gain maximum independence in daily living activities. Write them on the chart under "Needs to Learn" in the order of importance to your student. Also record the skills that you are working on, the date you began work, and the date your student accomplishes a skill. You can both be proud of this record of hard work and progress!

Begin working on the objects most crucial to your student's ability to function independently. Carry out these activities in natural settings (for example, brushing teeth after eating). Add some fun activities, such as work with toys—especially before and after you work on a task that is more difficult. A fun activity will help the student feel less frustrated and negative toward the difficult tasks.

Our students love to please us. Praise them for their efforts, and enjoy the time you share!

The Speech Staff

"CAN DO" CHART

Can Do

Needs to Learn

Skills Working On	Date Work Began	Date Accomplished

OBJECT TOOL USAGE

Learning to use objects as tools can help your student become more resourceful and independent at home and at school. By the word *tools,* we do not mean a hammer or screwdriver; we are talking about objects such as a string, a stick, a tray, or a chair. Here are four examples of how these common objects can help your student function more independently—and even learn to use real tools later on!

String
Tie a string, piece of yarn, or piece of rope to an attractive object or toy. Place the object in the student's sight, but out of reach. Help the student learn to pull the string, yarn, or rope to obtain the object. Vary the objects, and use different places. Commercially produced pull-toys also teach this skill.

Stick
Place a desirable object, toy, or food item on the table within the student's sight, but out of reach. Give the student a stick, pencil, or other tool. Help the student use the tool to move the object until it is within reach and the student can grasp it.

Tray
Place a desirable object, toy, or food item on a tray, piece of paper, or sheet of cardboard. Put the tray, paper, or cardboard within the student's reach, but place the object beyond reach. Help the student attain the desired object by pulling the tray until the object is within reach.

Chair

While the student is watching, place a desirable object on a shelf or area that is too high for the student to reach. Help the student push a chair or stool to the area and climb up and obtain the object. (Be sure that the shelf or area is not too high and that the chair or stool is stable.)

Using the New Skill

Just because this skill is learned doesn't mean that the student should be given access to everything in your home or at school. The student also must learn how to use the skill appropriately. Controls and limitations must be set and adhered to. Imagine, for example, that the cookie jar is placed out of reach and the student uses a chair to try to get at the cookies after being told "No." Consistent behavior management is essential. Do not allow the student to use the chair. Redirect the student's attention to another activity. If you have been using a cookie as a reward, change to a different treat.

Please let us know of any different tools you have used in teaching this skill, so we can share ideas with other parents.

The Speech Staff

ACQUIRING ADULT ATTENTION

Frequently, youngsters have difficulty developing an appropriate means of gaining an adult's attention. Often they use an inappropriate or disruptive behavior, such as turning or grabbing the adult's face, crying, banging, hitting or performing another inappropriate behavior that has gained attention in the past. (Unfortunately, adults often reinforce these behaviors by giving them more attention than appropriate behaviors.)

In addition to structuring more reinforcement (love, hugs, and pats) for good behavior, we can teach an appropriate way of gaining adult attention. Nonverbal students can be taught to tap others on the shoulder or arm when seeking attention. This natural gesture is used in classrooms everywhere—and yet we forget to teach it to our handicapped youngsters!

Practice this activity by having an adult hold a desirable object while avoiding eye contact and interaction with the youngster. A second adult helps the student approach and tap the first adult on the arm or shoulder to gain both the adult's attention and access to the desirable object.

Students who can verbally call others by name should be encouraged to do so when trying to gain attention. Students with emerging verbal skills should attempt to say a person's name as well as tap the arm or shoulder.

These are natural and appropriate ways for gaining attention. Using them in everyday activities will enhance your student's communication and social skills.

The Speech Staff

IMITATION

Learning to imitate can be fun! Many games and records teach this skill.

We will discuss two kinds of imitation—imitation involving the use of objects, and imitation involving the use of body parts.

Imitation with Objects

In learning to imitate using objects, a wide variety of items may be used. Some examples are:

Scribbling on paper with a pencil or crayon
Stacking blocks or rings
Ringing a bell or hitting a drum
Putting a hat on and taking it off
Using a paper towel to dry hands
Using a tissue or napkin
Pushing a toy car
Combing hair
Blowing bubbles
Rolling, throwing, or bouncing a ball

Demonstrate the action with an object. Then, have the student imitate what you are doing.

The next skill—using objects functionally—is likely to develop quickly. This will greatly improve your youngster's ability to function independently.

Imitation with Body Parts

Motor imitation skills are essential for students who are using sign language; and practical skills, such as washing the face and hands, can be enhanced by practice involving imitation of motor acts.

Simple games like peek-a-boo and pat-a-cake incorporate imitation of actions involving body parts. Finger plays and songs such as "Put Your Finger In the Air" also teach motor imitation. Present the action and have the student imitate what you are doing. Think of ways to have fun while you practice these skills!

The Speech Staff

MATCHING

Matching is a learning skill that eventually leads to symbolic representation, the concept that a symbol (word, picture, sign, etc.) can represent an object, thought, or idea. Matching also is important because it is used often in prevocational and vocational tasks.

We will discuss three basic levels of matching: matching objects, matching objects to pictures, and matching pictures.

Matching Objects

The most basic matching task is that of matching identical objects. To teach this skill, typically we place three objects on the table (for example, a shoe, a comb, and a plate). Then we hold up an object that matches one of the items on the table, and direct the student to find it. Sometimes we give the object and have the student place it on top of or beside the matching object. At other times, we hold the object in one hand and hold out the other hand while requesting that the student find and give the matching item. Common household items—shoes, spoons, cups, and toothbrushes—are ideal objects to use in this activity.

Once a student can match paired identical objects, the next step is to match pairs of items that are not identical, such as a tennis shoe and a dress shoe, a measuring spoon and a regular spoon, a blue mug and a white cup. In this activity, the student demonstrates recognition that an object is the same regardless of variations in size, color, and sometimes even shape.

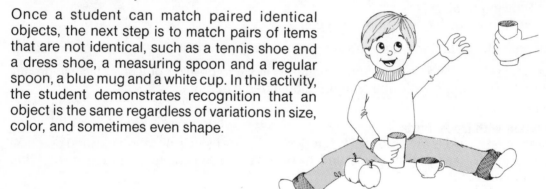

Matching Objects to Pictures

The next step is to teach your student to match real objects to pictures of that object. Magazine and catalog pictures are great to use with this activity. Present a choice of three pictures, then give the student a real object that matches one of the pictures. Help the student find the correct picture and place the object on it.

Time spent looking through magazines and catalogs for the pictures can be doubly useful if you name the objects aloud as you and your student look at the pictures.

Matching Identical Pictures

A more difficult matching task is that of matching pairs of pictures. Place three pictures on the table, present a fourth picture that matches one of the previous three, and direct the student to match it. At first, use identical pictures. Eventually, the student should be able to match nonidentical pairs of pictures, such as a tennis shoe and a dress shoe.

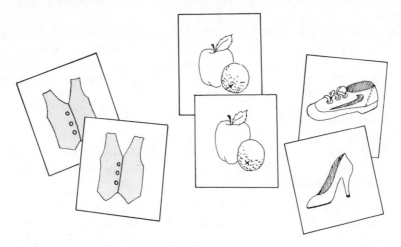

Practicing These Skills

In all of these matching activities, it is critical for the student to be able to visually scan (look at) all the items presented. At first, you may have to move the student's head, name each object, and say "Look at the (object)." Once the student can visually scan the items independently, a verbal reminder to look at all the items often is all that is needed.

Practice matching skills in daily living activities, such as cooking, setting the table, and dressing. Make matching activities in "Lotto" and other game formats. Just let your imagination go, and discover all the household items you can use to help your youngster learn to match!

The Speech Staff

REJECTING AND ACCEPTING OBJECTS

Some students passively accept any items given to them without seeming to show any preference or ability to reject unwanted items. Others are able to reject unwanted objects, but do so in a disruptive and undesirable way. We must teach our youngsters to refuse to accept items, such as inedible objects when eating, and to reject them in an acceptable manner.

Present several desirable objects—a piece of cookie, a candy, and some popcorn. Then offer the student a large inedible object, such as a shoe. Help the student reject the undesirable item by gently pushing your hand and the undesirable object away. You may also shake your head "no," help the student gesture "no," and say "No, thank you," to provide appropriate words to the student.

Toys also can be used to teach this skill. Present several desirable toys, then give the student an undesirable object, such as a towel. Help the student to gently push the towel away and gesture "no" with a head shake, while you say "No, I don't want the towel."

By teaching the student how to reject unwanted things in an acceptable manner, you are teaching not only the concept of rejection, but also more acceptable behavior. Your student may choose to use the new skill to manipulate you. For example, the student may reject some vegetables when you are serving dinner. If this happens, acknowledge the rejection by saying "I understand that you don't want your vegetable." Then set up a contingency: "But you must eat at least one bite before you can have dessert." Be consistent with your expectations, and do not allow the student to manipulate the situations by crying or tantruming. You may need to use further behavior management by removing the student from the dinner table, saying "We don't cry at the table when we are eating. When you are quiet, you may come back." When you bring the quieted student back to the table, repeat your expectation: "You may have your dessert when you have eaten one bite of vegetable." At first, you may have to remove the student from the table more than once. When the dinner hour is over, take away the food. If the student has not eaten the vegetable, do not give any dessert or other food until the next scheduled meal. You may want to praise others for eating their vegetable and reward them with dessert while the student watches. It may take some time for your student to understand that you cannot be manipulated. The effort will be worthwhile once your student learns to reject things in an acceptable manner and can deal with your authority. Ultimately, you will have a better behaved person who is more open to new things.

The Speech Staff

20

UNDERSTANDING "NO"

Learning to understand and respond appropriately to the command "No!" is crucial to all students' development. It may even affect their safety at some time. Imagine a youngster starting to eat something harmful. A serious accident might be averted if the student has learned to respond correctly to the command "No!"

One of the things we have to avoid is using "no" too much. If a student is constantly bombarded with "no," its importance is not understood. It is easy for teachers and parents to fall into the "nagging syndrome," where we nag and say "no" so frequently that interactions become negative and the meaning of "no" is lost.

To avoid this, we must first decide the types of situations that merit the command. Potentially harmful and dangerous situations, such as eating poisonous substances or running into the street, are examples of occurrences that merit the use of "No!" A serious and negative consequence must be imposed by a parent when a youngster has ignored a "no" command involving a potentially dangerous situation. Consistent behavior management and consequences are essential!

On the other hand, less serious situations are better served by using an alternate phrase, such as "It's not time to watch TV," combined with a redirection: "Let's play with the books instead." In this way, an unnecessary use of "no" and a negative interaction can be avoided while a new direction for a desirable and more productive activity is substituted.

With a little practice, the use of redirection in place of "No!" will become second nature to you, and the number of power struggles between you and your student should decrease. This should create more positive interactions, less nagging, and a better relationship between you.

The Speech Staff

GREETINGS

An important social skill involving communication is that of using "hello" and "good-bye." These greetings open the door for social interaction requiring eye contact, turn-taking, and physical interaction. Through this activity, positive experiences in communicating are established.

For a youngster who doesn't talk, a simple wave will do. For the verbal student, "hi" and "bye" or their approximations are good. A student who is just beginning to make speech sounds or is attempting to talk should be encouraged to make a verbal attempt and also to wave. Students who use an alternate communication system should be expected to express greetings using that system. Regardless of achievement level, it is important that your student makes eye contact with the person being greeted, and that a positive and warm exchange occurs between them.

Help your student practice using greetings when friends or family enter or leave your home. When out in the community, take advantage of numerous occasions in which your student can greet others. Older students may practice handshaking during greetings.

We hope this activity will lead much enjoyable social contact for your student.

The Speech Staff

FOLLOWING SIMPLE DIRECTIONS, REQUESTS, AND COMMANDS

Being able to understand and respond to simple directions, requests, and commands helps a youngster become better behaved, more attentive to the environment, and more capable of functioning independently. Directives commonly used at school include:

Sit down.	Give me the _____ .
Come here.	Touch the _____ .
Stand up.	Point to the _____ .
Put it here.	Get the _____ .
Put it there.	Go to the _____ .

You may choose to work on these requests or on others that are more relevant to your home needs. Work on one or two directives until your student demonstrates some consistency in following them. Gradually, add new directives. Practice these commands throughout the day in natural situations. Praise your student for successes, and try to avoid power struggles that escalate undesirable behaviors. Instead, try to catch your youngster being successful. For example, when your student sits at the table at mealtime, give praise: "I'm glad you are sitting here at the table. Now you can have some dinner." If your student does not respond to the directive, "Sit down," give praise to others for correct behavior and use them as an example. In this way, negative, noncompliant behavior is ignored. In order to get food, the youngster must be sitting and must follow your directive.

If this task is difficult, help your student to understand and carry out the directives. Give the student an idea of what you expect by repeating the procedure several times.

Once your student is able to carry out basic commands, you can begin to include more complex directives involving one to several objects, actions, or body parts. Some examples are:

Jump up!
Pick up the ball.
Shake your head.
Give me the toothpaste and toothbrush.
Open the door and turn off the lights.

It is important to make this activity enjoyable and relevant. Would you want to follow directions that were unpleasant, unrelated to our daily world, given in a negative tone of voice, or if we were not given any recognition for a job well done?

Our youngsters often seek to please us. They need to experience all of the positive aspects of communication in order to enhance their social and communication skills. Let's provide them with enjoyable tasks to improve their ability to follow simple directions!.

The Speech Staff

COMMUNICATING WANTS AND NEEDS

Those who cannot talk, sign, or use some formal system of alternate communication to express wants and needs often show their frustration by disruptive and inappropriate behavior. It is important to establish a simple communication system to help them express their wants and needs.

This skill can be taught at several levels. The first level is that of using an adult as a tool. Basically, our students are taught to take an adult by the hand and touch a desired or needed object. To get a youngster to this point, place the youngster's hand on top of your hand and help the youngster use the adult hand to point to or touch desired objects.

Once the students consistently use the adult hand to touch desired items, they are taught to touch or point to desirable items independently. To get your student to this point, you may need to reverse roles, using the student's hand as a tool immediately after the student has used your hand to request an object.

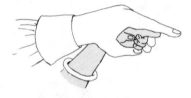

At first, the student may use the entire hand to touch or point to items. It is necessary to refine the touching or pointing, so that eventually the student can use the index finger to point to items. Teach this refinement by holding the student's index finger between your index finger and thumb and curling the remaining fingers under with your fingers.

To practice pointing skills, give your student a choice of three items, two that are not desirable and one that is highly desirable. When the student consistently points to the desirable item when given a choice, you can use this activity throughout the day to give your youngster choices of foods, toys, work activities, and even places to go. As the ability to communicate wants and needs increases, the less frustrated and the better behaved your student will be!

The Speech Staff

PLAY

Play is an important vehicle for learning. It can teach many valuable skills and concepts. Our youngsters sometimes need to be taught to play, even with the simplest toys. Basic play activities include manipulating busy-box toys, playing with bubbles, hitting a drum, rolling a ball, stacking rings, and pushing a toy car.

Once the student has mastered play with these simple toys, you can introduce others that involve more complicated operations. These include wind-up toys, push-and-go toys, and toys that are operated by manipulating a switch or turning on a battery. These toys teach the concept of *cause/effect*; that is, if an action is carried out (such as turning the key on a wind-up toy), it becomes a "cause," and the result, or "effect," is that something will happen. In this case, the toy will move.

At a higher level, play can involve the use of memory and imagination. Some toys that require many language concepts, memory, and imagination during play include dolls and dollhouses, puppets, building blocks, toy store items for shopping, and art supplies—paint, crayons, markers, scissors, paste, and clay.

While teaching your youngster to play with these more complicated toys, be sure to vary the play activities. For example, when playing with a doll and dollhouse, have the doll carry out a number of different activities, such as cooking, sleeping, and watching TV. When playing with building blocks, make different items—a house, bridge, or car. Always talk to your youngster while playing, regardless of the youngster's ability to respond verbally. Hearing your words will enhance understanding of words and language concepts.

The Speech Staff

IMAGINATIVE PLAY

Empty boxes and scraps of wood can become wonderful toys! With a little imagination, three wooden blocks can be a bridge for a car to drive over, and a box can become a garage. This kind of make-believe imaginative play, which requires one object to represent another object, is called *symbolic play.* It is the highest level of play in which a youngster can engage.

The following is an example of an adult and child playing house, using toys as well as imaginative play. The example demonstrates how the adult can describe the action. The youngster need only be willing to participate in the action (although verbal youngsters should be encouraged to express themselves at the highest level possible).

At first, the adult may need to manipulate the student through all the pretend activities. If the play routine is repeated often and is reinforced by similar real-life experiences, eventually the student should learn the basic sequence of steps involved in both the play and real-life activity.

Dishwashing

Situation: *The child and adult have just finished eating a pretend meal, using toy dishes. They are ready to play a pretend dishwashing activity.*

Materials: *Toy sink and dishes*

Adult: That lunch was really good. Now we need to wash the dishes. Let's go wash them.

*(The adult and child carry the dishes to the toy sink.
After placing the dishes in the sink, the child begins to wash them.)*

Adult: Don't we need some soap and water to wash the dishes?

(The adult and child pretend to turn on the water.)

Adult *(putting hand in water)*: Ouch! That's too hot! Let's add some cold water.

*(The child pretends to turn on cold water,
with the adult's help if needed.)*

Adult: We forgot to add the soap.

*(Both act out the motion of pouring soap.
The child puts the dishes into the pretend soapy water in the sink.)*

Adult: Now we have the dishes in the soapy water and we are ready to wash. Do you have a dishcloth? Here's one. You wash them really clean, and I'll rinse them with some clear water.

(The child hands the dishes to the adult, who pretends to rinse them.)

Adult: Before we put the dishes away, we have to dry them. Here are two dishtowels—one for you and one for me.

(Both pretend to dry dishes.)

Adult (pretending to drop a dish): Oh, look what happened! I had an accident. I dropped a dish, and it is broken all over the floor. Now I have to clean up the mess. Would you get the broom and dustpan?

*(The child brings the pretend broom and dustpan.
The adult may need to help the child "find" the pretend items.)*

Adult: I'll sweep and you hold the dustpan. Be careful! Don't get cut on the broken dish.

(The adult may need to demonstrate actions for the child.)

Adult: Let's put the broken dish in the garbage.

(Both pretend to throw away the broken pieces.)

Adult: Let's finish drying the dishes and putting them away.

(Both pretend to dry the dishes and put them away.)

Adult (naming each item as it is put into the cupboard): This is a cup. You find a cup.

(The child picks up a cup and attempts to say "cup.")

Adult: You found the cup—and you even *said* "cup." Good job!

Adult (summarizing the play): We did a good job washing and drying the dishes and putting them away. We are good workers.

During this brief imaginary play activity, some of the ideas and concepts presented are:

    The natural sequence of dishwashing
    The natural sequence of sweeping, using a dustpan and garbage can
    Dirty and clean dishes
    Wet and *dry* dishes
    Hot and *cold* water
    Turning faucets *off* and *on*
    Using soap and water to wash
    Using clear water to rinse
    Using a towel to dry
    Putting objects *in* and *on* other objects
    Safety (getting burned or cut)
    Making mistakes and taking responsibility for them
    Cleaning up messes
    Helping others
    Putting items away
    Labeling items and telling their uses

As you can see, this type of imaginary play activity has the potential to teach many useful skills. Youngsters who have more expressive skills, either through speech or the use of an alternate communication system, should be encouraged to communicate at whatever level they are capable. This might include naming or requesting objects, actions, locations, using phrases or sentences, and even asking questions. The adult can expand on the youngster's actions or expressions and can correct any language structures or concepts that are not accurate.

It is important to allow your youngster some independence in play, yet still provide some structure and the language concepts involved in the activity. In this casual learning situation, the youngster has the opportunity to gain many new ideas and learn better communication skills.

Share imaginative play often, and see your youngster's communication skills grow!

The Speech Staff

Receptive Language

OBJECT AND PICTURE RECOGNITION

Two basic activities used in language therapy involve recognizing common objects and recognizing pictures of objects. There are many fun and easy ways you can help your student practice these skills at home. Begin by placing three objects on the table. Select objects that allow you to act out or demonstrate their use, such as a comb (pretend to comb hair), a cup (pretend to drink) or a ball (pretend to throw). Make sure the student looks at all three objects. Say, "Find the (object)" while you perform the gesture that demonstrates the object's use. Gradually decrease the use of gestures until the student can recognize the objects with only the verbal direction, "Find the (object)." For students on a sign language program, the signs should be used with all verbal directions in every activity. To make this activity a game, let your student use a puppet to "Find the (object)."

Another fun activity is playing "store." Let the student be the clerk, while you use tokens, poker chips, play money, or pennies to buy items the student correctly selects.

Treasure hunts and scavenger hunts are fun, too. Scatter a few toy animals within several feet of the student. Then have the student "hunt" for specific animals. Have a treasure hunt, using objects of a specific category, such as clothing, or objects from several categories.

Before learning to recognize pictures of objects, the student must be able to match objects to pictures. Select a few pictures of common objects the student already recognizes. Also place the corresponding objects on the table. Say, "Find the (object)." Then have the student "Put it on the picture of (object). Match it." When the student has matched all three objects to the three pictures, remove the objects and say, "Find the picture of (object)." As the routine becomes familiar, gradually eliminate the matching task. Again, a puppet or doll can be used to make this activity fun.

Use magazines or catalogs to "Find the picture of (object)." Have the student cut out pictures to make a book or a picture collage. This activity involves the fine motor skills of cutting and pasting as well as the language skill of following directions.

Other activities can include the use of paper dolls, color forms, or large posters. Direct the student to "Find the (doll's coat)" or "Look at the poster and find the (chair)." Try to use familiar games, toys, objects, and materials in your picture recognition activities.

Choose relevant items that will increase your student's ability to function independently. It is far more important to teach your youngster to recognize hygiene items, such as soap and toothbrush, than it is to teach about zoo animals. Help your student recognize household objects, familiar people, clothing, foods, and body parts; and work on less critical vocabulary later.

It also is important for you to expect a certain level of performance in eye contact, sitting, attending, and compliance; and for you to praise and reward all efforts. If you choose relevant vocabulary, expect good behavior, and give frequent praise, you can use any one of hundreds of activities to teach object and picture recognition. Enjoy a variety of activities often!

The Speech Staff

RECOGNIZING OBJECTS AND PICTURES BY THEIR USES

Being able to recognize objects when given their use is a functional skill that enhances students' independence. Place three objects on the table. These must be objects your student recognizes. Say, "Find the one you (function) with." If the student has difficulty understanding the function or action word, you may need to act out or pantomime how the object is used. Gradually eliminate the use of pantomime as the student's skill increases. A doll or puppet may be used to increase the enjoyment of this activity.

Another fun activity involves helping your student recognize the *wrong* functions of objects. For example, use a spoon and act out combing your hair. Ask, "Do we comb our hair with a spoon?" Give help if the student is unable to indicate "no." Then say, "Find the one we comb our hair with." Students enjoy the silliness of this activity while also learning "yes" and "no."

Carry out these activities in natural situations throughout the day. For example, say, "It's time to brush your teeth. Find the one you need to brush your teeth with." When naming objects around the house, tell and demonstrate their uses so the student will learn to recognize the objects by their functions.

Use picture cards, magazines, and catalogs to teach recognition of pictured objects when given their functions. For example, while looking at pictures of silverware and dishes from a magazine or catalog, ask the student to "Find the one we (drink) from." At a more complex level, present picture cards from two categories, such as food and toys. Say, "Find the ones we eat" and have the student place the food pictures in one container and "the ones we play with" in a second container. (Before beginning this activity, make sure your student can find single pictures when told a function.)

Our students often seek to please us and gain our approval. Reward them for their hard work with lots of affection, and enjoy the times you share!

The Speech Staff

UNDERSTANDING ACTIONS AND VERBS

Verbs, or action words, are a very necessary part of communication. Understanding common action verbs is essential to the student's ability to follow directions and comprehend what others are saying.

Activities that teach students to understand basic actions can be carried out in so many fun ways. The game of "Simon Says" may be used to give action commands, even though the student may not fully understand the concept involved. If the student has difficulty with the game, you may wish to say only "Show me how you (action)."

Practice action concepts in natural situations throughout the day. For example, direct the student to "brush your teeth" after a meal. To make the activity more enjoyable, have the student use a bendable doll or puppet to carry out the action.

Once the student can carry out action commands, introduce exercises that teach the students to recognize actions in pictures. Place three action pictures on the table, and say "Find the picture of (action)." You may have a doll give the directions, or the student can use a puppet to find the action pictures.

Photographs of your student, family members, friends, and pets may be used to make action books or an action picture collage. Magazines, children's storybooks, and coloring books contain many action pictures.

Choose relevant actions that your student experiences in everyday activities. Be sure to make the exercises fun and enjoyable—and don't forget to praise your student for hard work!

The Speech Staff

UNDERSTANDING LOCATIONS AND PREPOSITIONS

Locations indicate places. Noun places tell where an object or item is placed or located. *Prepositions* are more specific locations that tell the relationship between two objects. For example, in the sentence, "The car is in the garage," *garage* is the noun location, and *in* is the preposition—the specific location that indicates the exact relationship between the car and the garage.

To help your student learn noun locations, present an object and direct the student to put it in a location (for example, "Hat, head" or "Put hat on head"). Once the student can place objects in their usual location, give directions involving unusual locations (for example, "Hat, floor" or "Put hat on floor").

When the student can follow these noun location directions, begin to add basic pairs of prepositions to the commands, teaching one pair at a time. *In/out, on/off, over/under,* and *up/down* usually are learned first. Later, students acquire *in front of/in back of* or *behind, beside* or *next to,* and *between.* Teach only one pair of prepositions at a time. Practice giving prepositional commands using real objects or toys. For example, when playing with the dollhouse, dolls, and furniture, direct the student or "the doll" to carry out the prepositional commands.

Integrate the use of prepositions during daily activities. For example, when setting the table, direct the student to put the placemat *on* the table, the fork *on* the napkin, the knife and spoon *beside* the plate, and the saucer *under* the cup. During laundry chores, have the student put clothes *in* and take them *out* of the washer and dryer.

Once the student has learned to understand prepositions using real objects, begin to introduce pictures that illustrate spatial relationships. Children's storybooks and coloring books often depict objects and people in varied positions. Magazines are another source of pictures. Commercial materials also are available to teach prepositions.

You will find lots of ways to teach locations and prepositions. Many of these "lessons" can include household chores and daily living activities that also help your student become more independent.

These concepts are difficult to learn because they are abstract. Praise all efforts, and help your student experience success in learning to understand locations and prepositions.

The Speech Staff

UNDERSTANDING TWO-WORD AND THREE-WORD PHRASES

First, students learn to understand the names of objects, and then they learn to recognize independent action words. Once these basic comprehension tasks are accomplished with common objects and actions, students must learn to understand when these concepts are combined in one phrase. One way to practice this skill is to use small toys such as miniature animals, dollhouse furniture, and small figures of people. Place a toy dog on one toy chair, and a second toy animal, a horse, on a different chair. Put a third figure, another dog, on the bed. Say "Find (the) dog sitting." The student must discriminate between a dog and a horse, and also between the actions *sitting* and *sleeping.* Then present toy animals and furniture, and direct the student to "Show me (the) dog sitting."

Once the student is able to follow these directions using toy animals, begin to use figures of people. You may need to practice recognizing males (first name of a male family member, then Daddy, man, boy) and females (first name of a female family member, then Mama, woman, girl). Enlist family members to help the student practice recognizing male and female figures. Ask them to carry out various actions while directing the student to "Find (the) girl combing." When the student can discriminate between male and female figures, place the toy figures in varied positions in the dollhouse. Place one male and one female figure in the same position, sitting. Put a third figure in a different action position, sleeping. Say "Find (the) Mama sitting." After the student recognizes the two components of person or object and action, you may add a third part to the phrase; for example, "(The) girl (is) sitting (on the) chair" or "(The) boy (is) sleeping (on the) sofa." Practice these skills until your student can recognize two- and three-word phrases while using objects.

Students who recognize simple pictures may practice this skill using two pictures that have one similarity and a third that has nothing in common with one of the other two. For example, present one picture of a girl eating, a second picture of a girl combing her hair, and a third picture of a boy eating. Say "Find (the) boy eating." The student must discriminate between the girl and boy. If you say "Find (the) girl combing," the student then must discriminate between eating and combing. Add a third component to phrases when the student recognizes two-word phrases when they are illustrated in pictures. Magazines, coloring books, children's books, and catalogs are good sources for these pictures.

As your student becomes more skilled at understanding two-word and three-word phrases, the ability to understand and follow directions also will improve. The comprehension of basic words and their relationship is essential to your student's communication development.

The Speech Staff

UNDERSTANDING ADJECTIVES: SIZE, COLOR, AND NUMBER

In describing objects, we use adjectives to tell size, color, and number. Many relevant activities, materials, and objects found around home and school can be used to teach common adjectives.

Size

Learning to tell the difference between big and little can be done in so many fun ways. One particularly enjoyable activity is having the student find *big* and *little* pieces of food. Place two small pieces of cookie and one large piece on the table. Say, "Find and eat the big cookie," or "Give a little cookie to me." Once the student knows the difference between big and little foods, introduce bowls, cups, spoons, utensils, and other kitchen items that vary in size. Practice finding big and little items while cooking, setting the table, and cleaning the kitchen. Generalize the skill to other areas of daily living, such as sorting and folding laundry. Always present three items. More than three may be overwhelming, and a two-item choice gives a 50% chance of guessing the right answer.

Once your student becomes skilled at identifying big and little objects, teach the concept of big and little by using pictures. A fun activity involves using a large posterboard elephant and a small posterboard mouse. Present pictures of big and little items, and have the student place the large items on the elephant and the small items on the mouse. For a variation, have the student attach the pictures to the posters with Velcro or clothespins.

Color

Although color recognition is often drilled by parents and teachers, actually it is a highly overrated skill in terms of importance to a youngster's learning—but it's fun! Present the concept in casual situations throughout the day. For example, while sorting the laundry, present three objects that vary in color only, such as a red, a blue, and a yellow sock. Direct the student to "Find the red sock." You may have to give an association: "An apple is red. Find the one that is the same color as an apple."

If learning color recognition is particularly difficult, first have the student sort items by color while you say the color label for each item. When the sorting task is completed, as the student to "Find the (color) object."

Constructing color unit books can become a favorite activity. Choose a color, and paste an object to represent that color on the cover of the book. For example, use an apple on the cover of the Red book. Help your student look in magazines or catalogs for pictures of red items. Then cut them out and paste them on paper. Assemble the book and attach the pages inside the cover.

Whatever color activities you share with your youngster, make them enjoyable and carry them out in casual situations throughout the day.

Number

Number concepts are very important to many aspects of learning and independent functioning. To begin, ask the student to give you one to five items. Help the student place the items, one at a time, into a container as you count. Use a gesture, such as putting your hand in the air or over the container, to indicate when the specified number is reached and the student may stop adding items. Practice this exercise until the student gives only the specified number of items. Make up cards containing the numerals 1 to 5, and mark one to five spaces on which to place the objects. This will help your student understand the number concepts and the functional counting tasks. Once the student can give up to five items on request, increase the numbers gradually to ten objects, and eventually to twenty or more.

When the student can recognize and understand number concepts to ten using objects, begin to introduce pictured items that vary in number. Say, "Find the picture of *three* spoons." If the student experiences difficulty, present objects to match the pictures; and gradually fade their use as the student's skill increases.

Practice counting skills throughout the day in daily living activities. Relevant exercises—like counting the number of forks, knives, or spoons needed to set the table—make learning number concepts more significant and useful.

The Speech Staff

UNDERSTANDING OPPOSITE ADJECTIVES

Adjectives that describe objects, places, or people often are taught in opposite pairs, so students can compare and contrast. The following are some examples of practical ways to teach opposite concepts while going through the daily routine.

Hot/Cold

Take your student near the kitchen stove or oven that has cooled but is still slightly warm. Hold the student's hand at a safe distance, and let the youngster feel the warmth. Say, "The stove is hot! We don't touch it or we'll get burned." If your student is too active for this activity, use a heating pad, warming tray, heater vent, or other warm object to teach *hot*. Then introduce the concept of *cold* by taking the student to the refrigerator or freezer to feel the cold. Teach these concepts using hot and cold water faucets, hot or cold food, and even snow in contrast to the heat inside the house.

Big/Little

Many big and little items around the house can be used to teach these concepts. One of the most motivating is to offer *big* or *little* portions of food. Use cooking utensils, such as measuring spoons, bowls, and cups that come in varied sizes. Have your youngster point to big and little items on request. Laundry folding is another good activity for teaching big and little. Have your student place the big socks in one pile and the little ones in another pile.

Clean/Dirty

These concepts can be taught easily while doing dishes or washing clothes. Point to the soil, and say "This is dirty!" Once the student has washed the item, point to the area where the dirt was, and say "There's no dirt. It's clean." Have the student point out clean and dirty items around the house as you do household chores.

Wet/Dry

Teach these concepts in the same activities as *clean* and *dirty*.

Happy/Sad

When your student is showing these emotions, provide the name for the emotion. Point out emotions others are showing in real situations or when you are watching a movie or TV show. Discuss actions that are appropriate for the various emotions: "Johnny is happy. Look at him laughing. Mary is sad. Look at her face. She is crying." Have your student indicate people or point to pictures of people showing the emotions *happy* and *sad*.

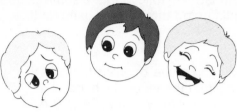

Empty/Full

Point out containers around the house that are *full*. Then show the student that once the contents are used, the containers are *empty*. Do this with soup cans, packaged mixes, frozen juice mixes, and the student's own plate or cup before and after eating. Have the student show or point to containers that are full or empty.

Hard/Soft and Smooth/Rough

Help the student find objects around the house that have various surfaces and textures. While the student touches or feels the objects, provide labels: "The pillow is soft, the floor is hard" or "The wall is smooth, the sandpaper is rough."

Long/Short and Tall/Short

Many objects around the house illustrate these concepts. When cleaning carrots, point out the various sizes by saying, "Here's a long carrot. See how big it is." Then present a short carrot, and say, "This carrot is short. See how little it is." When folding clothes, compare adult-sized pants or socks to child-sized items. To teach the concept of tall, compare family members' height, showing who is tallest and who is shortest. Help your student recognize and point to *long*, *tall*, and *short* objects and people in the environment.

Other Opposite Adjectives

Many other pairs of opposite describing words can be taught during daily routines. Some of these are *fat/thin*, *light/dark*, *pretty/ugly*, *sweet/sour*, *good/bad*, and *fast/slow*. Use these and other describing words, and help your student understand the difference between the terms.

The Speech Staff

UNDERSTANDING "SAME" AND "DIFFERENT"

The ability to recognize likenesses and differences in objects is basic to many learning tasks. These concepts originate within matching tasks where an object is presented with the directive, "Find one like this." The student is then presented with a choice of several objects, one of which is the same as the first object. This skill must be mastered before the student can progress to the more complex activity of determining likenesses and differences as being the *same* or *different*.

Begin teaching the concepts of *same* and *different* with a sorting task. Place two boxes or containers on the table. Present several items that are identical and one other that is different. Help the student sort the items by placing the *same* items in one box and the *different* object in the other box. As the student is sorting, say, "This one is a cup, and that one is a cup, too. They look alike. They're both the same." As the different object is placed in the box, tell the student, "That one's a ball. It is not a cup. It is different." Then say, "Give me the ones that are the same" or "Give me the one that is different." If the student needs further clues, you might use the numbers one and two to indicate two items that are the same or one item that is different. Practice until the student spontaneously gives you the requested items without any clues.

Sorting socks is an excellent way to practice using the concepts of same and different. Not only is it relevant; it also helps the student participate in household tasks. Sorting silverware, buttons, nuts and bolts, and many other household items are tasks that require no special materials. Integrate these activities into your daily routine, and see how quickly your student masters the concepts of same and different. Give praise often, and make sure the student enjoys the activities and experiences.

The Speech Staff

41

UNDERSTANDING COMPARISONS OF SIZE, QUANTITY, AND QUALITY

Measuring and comparing the size and quantity of objects is an activity that can be used often in daily routines. When measuring cooking ingredients, for example, ask your student to "Bring the *biggest* cup" or "Find the *smallest* spoon." Show objects of three graduated sizes, such as ½ teaspoon, 1 teaspoon, and 1 tablespoon, and ask the student to "Find the *smallest* one." Present two different sized objects, and ask, "Which is the *bigger* one?" Comparison of size adjectives can be used while cooking, serving foods, cleaning, doing laundry, and carrying out many other household chores.

Teach the comparison of *more, most,* and *least* by giving varied quantities of food when serving, and then asking "Who has the most milk?" or "Who has the least to drink?" Direct your student to give one family member "a few peanuts" and another family member "many" or "lots" of peanuts. At first, you may need to use numbers to explain the concepts, such as "Two is a few and ten is many."

The concepts of *tall* and *short* also can be taught by comparisons: "Daddy is the tallest person in the family while baby Tim is the shortest." Comparisons of weight can be made, using the terms *light/heavy* or *fat/thin.*

For color comparisons, use the terms *light* and *dark.* This also teaches the concept of comparisons in situations other than in size and quantity. Other types of comparisons may include many pairs of opposite adjectives, such as *wet/dry, happy/sad, fast/slow,* and *clean/dirty.* These comparisons are more difficult to discriminate, so they should not be introduced until the student understands the basics of how to compare by size and quantity.

Comparisons of size and quantity also may be made while playing with various sizes of containers in sand, water, or corn tables. Serving "foods" to dolls or puppets may include giving "a few" cookies to one doll while the other gets "many."

Whatever the situation, be sure that teaching occurs in a pleasant, relaxed, and natural setting, so your student is less likely to be resistive to the activity and more likely to carry newly gained knowledge into other situations.

The Speech Staff

CLASSIFICATION AND CATEGORIZATION

Understanding how to group or sort items by similarities (for example, by their function or use) is called categorization. Students must recognize these similarities among items, a task that requires a high level of mental organization. It is a skill that is often used in workshops and skill centers, so students' abilities in this area will greatly affect their potential in a workshop setting.

To begin categorization by function, choose a number of items from two different categories, such as foods and clothing. Use empty food containers, plastic fruits and vegetables, miniature foods, real clothing items, or doll clothes. Present two containers, such as a grocery bag and a laundry basket, into which the foods and clothing must be sorted. Give an example by choosing a food item, and saying "This is soup. We eat it. It is a food. Foods go in the shopping bag." Then present a clothing item, and say, "This is a shirt. We wear it. It is clothing. We put it in the laundry basket." Then give food and clothing items randomly, and help the student sort them into the proper containers. You may also use pictures from specific categories and have the student sort them into the appropriate piles. Catalogs are good picture resources, because they usually have a number of pictures from a category on the same page.

Another categorization skill involves pictures containing several items from the same category. For example, one picture might showing an apple, a sandwich, and a cookie; a second one might show a woman, a child, and a man; and a third picture could show a chair, a sofa, and a table. Have the student look at these picture sets and, if able, label each item and tell its function. If the student is not able to express at this level, provide the information by naming the items and telling their uses. Say, "Look at the pictures and find the food." As the student becomes more skilled in recognizing the basic categories, you can introduce subcategories (for example, the food category can be broken down to fruits, vegetables, and meats).

Practice categorization skills often, using a variety of household materials and common objects. Vary the activities and the ways in which the sorting is carried out. This will give your student the ability to generalize categorization skills into a number of settings.

The Speech Staff

ASSOCIATION

Matching things that go together, such as a sock, shoe, and foot, is called association. Begin practicing this skill by presenting a choice of three objects. Hold up a fourth object that is related to one of the three on the table, and ask your student to find the one "that goes with this" or "is used with this." Help the student see the association by demonstrating how the two objects are related (for example, a saucer goes under a cup, a lid goes on a jar, or a lace goes in a shoe). Choose familiar functional objects, and point out the associations between them during your daily routine.

Once the student has mastered object association, introduce pictures of things that go together. Go-together card games, lottos, puzzles, and other commercial materials are available; and you can make a variety of aids that teach this skill. Workbooks at the preschool, kindergarten, and first grade level often contain sheets of go-together activities that can be cut up and made into picture cards. Magazine and catalog pictures also can be cut and glued to index cards. Present a choice of three picture cards, then hold up a fourth card and say, "Find the one that goes with this." Help the student understand the relationship between the two items by explaining how they are associated.

Use a variety of materials and experiences to teach association while sharing some fun activities. Remember to praise your student for a job well done!

The Speech Staff

UNDERSTANDING "IS" AND "IS NOT"

A negative statement using the word "not" is often difficult for our youngsters to understand. In order to teach this concept, the student must have some understanding of "no" and be able to sort things that are the "same" from things that are "different."

Choose several pairs of common objects your student already recognizes. Present three objects, two that are identical and one that is different (for example, two cups and a shoe). You may need to have the student practice finding the objects that are the "same" and the one that is "different." Then direct the student to "Find the one that is *not* a cup." If the student chooses a cup, say "No, I don't want the cup. I want the one that is different, the one that is *not* a cup." Demonstrate a sorting task by placing all the cups in one container, saying "cup" for each one, then saying "They are the same." When a different item is chosen, place it in a separate container saying, "No, it's *not* a cup. It's different. It's a shoe."

Once the student is able to carry out this task using objects, present sets of picture cards, two that are the same and one that is different. Carry out the activity in the same way you did with real objects. As the student learns to understand the negative "not" as related to pictured objects, you may introduce the concept with action pictures. Present two action pictures depicting sleeping and a third eating. Ask the student to "Find the one that is *not* sleeping."

Practice these activities throughout the day in as many natural situations as possible. Make the practice fun by presenting silly choices, such as two shoes and a box of cereal, and saying "You can eat the one that is *not* a shoe." Point out other people's activities, using "not" statements: "Mike is *not* running. He is walking."

Through frequent practice in varied situations, your student will gain understanding of this abstract concept of negation and "not." Remember to practice often, make the exercises enjoyable, and praise your student for hard work!

The Speech Staff

RECOGNIZING OBJECTS NEEDED FOR ROUTINE TASKS

Being able to recognize objects needed to carry out routine tasks is a skill that is important to students' independence. Before they can be able to make a sandwich, wash clothes, or clean, they must know and recognize the objects needed to carry out the tasks.

There are many activities you can use to practice this skill. For example, before making lunch, place all the items necessary for making the sandwich on the counter. Add several items that are not needed, such as a bar of soap, a pan, a comb, and a pencil. Ask the student to choose or give you everything needed to make a sandwich. Help the student choose all—and only—the items needed. Once this activity can be carried out with all the items on the counter, help the student find the items in their storage places instead of the counter. Tell the location of the items if needed: "Get a plate out of the cupboard" or "You can find the lunch meat in the refrigerator."

Practice this skill as part of your daily routine—when brushing teeth, dressing, bathing, making a simple breakfast or lunch, and wiping the table. First have the student choose the items needed to carry out the activity from those you have already made available. Later, help the student find the items in their usual storage places. Continue to add tasks as the student becomes more able to recognize items needed to carry out familiar chores.

You may want to have your youngster prepare a visual reminder of the items needed for carrying out a specific task. Help the student find magazine, newspaper, or catalog pictures of all items needed to complete the task. Have the student cut them out, glue them to cards, and place the cards on a ring. As each item is assembled, the student can turn the card to another picture. As the student becomes more skilled in carrying out the sequence of actions, the visual reminder can be faded.

Remember to give praise for hard work and acknowledge your student's growing independence!

The Speech Staff

UNDERSTANDING SINGULAR AND PLURAL

When referring to more than one object, we use a plural form of the item, usually by adding an "s" or "es." Students must be able to hear and recognize the difference in sound between the singular and plural forms.

An easy way to practice this skill is to put three or more spoons on the table, and ask the student to "Give me spoon" or "Give me spoons." If the student experiences difficulty, use the numbers "one" with "spoon" and "two" or "three" with "spoons." Once the student is able to carry out the task using the number clue, you can gradually fade the use of these clues.

There are lots of fun ways you can incorporate the concepts of singular and plural into your youngster's play. For example, you can play "store." If your youngster is able to work well with pictures, use them to practice comprehension of singular and plural.

Irregular plurals are formed by changes in spelling other than by adding "s" or "es." For example, leaf, knife, and foot all require changes in spelling when pluralizing to become leaves, knives, and feet. The student will learn to recognize irregular plurals through use and drill. Place pairs of picture cards on the table, one card showing one object and the other card showing several of the same object. Add a third card with a picture that is unrelated to the others. Ask your student to "Show me feet" or "Show me foot."

Make sure your youngster enjoys the activities, and vary the ways in which you practice. Integrate these exercises into the daily routine, and praise your student for a job well done!

The Speech Staff

MONEY

Recognizing coins and learning their values are functional and important skills for any youngster to learn. An easy way to teach coin recognition is to place three different coins on the table. It is good to start with a penny, a dime, and a quarter because of the contrast in size and color. Ask your student to "Find the (coin)." You may use a clue, such as "It's the brown one" or "We use it in the gum machine" for the penny, and "It's the big one we use in the video games" for the quarter. When you use a gum machine or video game, name the appropriate coin and give your student the opportunity to choose it.

Another way to teach coin recognition is to "pay" your student for daily chores or for completing work tasks. With the money earned, the student will be able to buy privileges or treats. Select privileges and treats that are highly motivating. The cost of these rewards should be established, and a time should be scheduled to see if the student has earned enough money. The length of wait should be determined by the individual's ability to attend to work and wait for the reward. Some students may be able to wait until the end of a day to receive their earned reward, while others may be able to wait for only brief periods. When that time comes, if the required amount has not been earned, the student *must* miss out on the reward. You may need to remind the student that the proper amount must be earned in order to get the reward. Encourage the student to try again.

Another fun way to learn to recognize coins is by playing "store." Gather a number of empty milk and egg cartons, cracker and cereal boxes, and soup and juice cans. Attach price stickers to the containers, using amounts under ten cents. Help the student buy items and count out the appropriate coins. Increase the cost of items as the student becomes more skilled at counting out the smaller amounts.

See pages 49-56 for Coin Value Worksheets #1-#8. Cut apart the money strips, and use them to teach your student how to count out six pennies to get six cents or how to combine the values of two coins, a nickel and a penny, to get this same sum. Have the student place actual coins over the pictures on the strips. Eventually, the student should be able to count out the coins without using the strips.

Once the student can count out small amounts of money and recognize the basic coins, you can begin to rehearse buying a favorite treat at the store. Buy several of the item yourself, and have the student practice making the purchase and paying the cashier at home. When the student is comfortable with the routine, you can make actual trips to the store to buy the item. If your student is able to add coin values and read, expanded the activity to include a small shopping list.

Please let us know any new and exciting ways you use for practicing this skill, so we can share it with other parents.

The Speech Staff

Coin Value Worksheet #1

1¢ =

2¢ =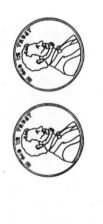

3¢ =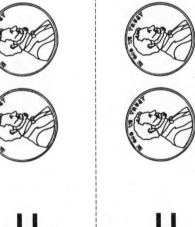

4¢ =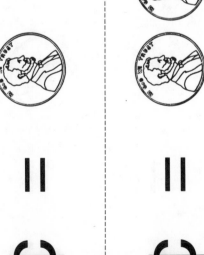

Coin Value Worksheet #2

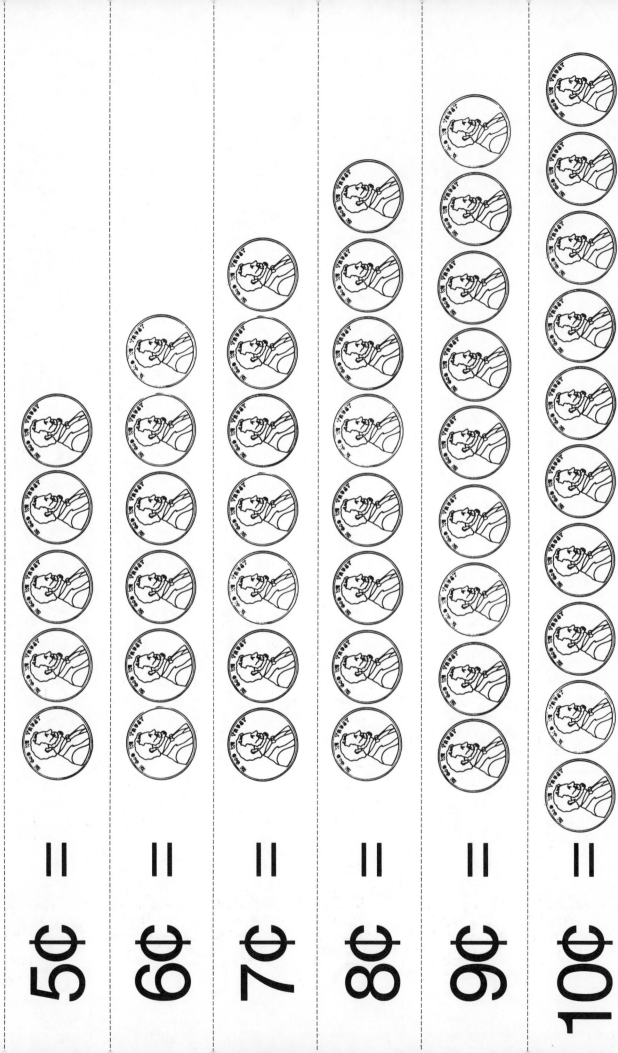

5¢ =

6¢ =

7¢ =

8¢ =

9¢ =

10¢ =

Coin Value Worksheet #3

5¢ =

6¢ =

7¢ =

8¢ =

9¢ =

10¢ =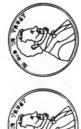

10¢ =

11¢ =

12¢ =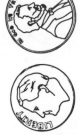

13¢ =

14¢ =

Coin Value Worksheet #5

15¢ =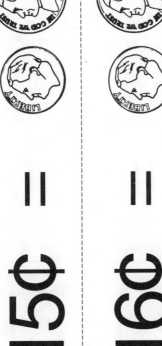

16¢ =

17¢ =

18¢ =

19¢ =

Coin Value Worksheet #6

$20¢ =$

$21¢ =$

$22¢ =$

$23¢ =$

$24¢ =$

$25¢ =$

Coin Value Worksheet #7

25¢ =

50¢ =

75¢ =

$1.00 =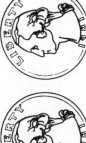

Coin Value Worksheet #8

50¢ =

75¢ =

$1.00 =

UNDERSTANDING WH QUESTIONS

Different questions require different kinds of answers. For example, *what* questions require the name of an object or action as an answer, *who* questions are answered with the names of people, and *where* questions are correctly answered with locations. Students must learn to discriminate between the different question words, and then must choose answers from the correct category. Pictures or objects may be used to teach question comprehension in many different learning activities.

What Questions
Present several common objects, such as a toothbrush, a comb, and a bar of soap. Ask simple *what* questions, such as "What do you wash with?" or "What do you use to clean your teeth with?" Help the student choose the correct object. Pictures may be used in this activity also.

Who Questions
Ask *who* questions about familiar people in the environment, such as "Who is standing up?" or "Who is watching TV?" Help the student find and point to the correct person. Photos of familiar people are excellent materials for this activity.

Where Questions
Place a few objects around the room while the student watches. Ask *where* questions, such as "Where is the ball?" Help the student point to the correct location of the object. Magazine pictures are good materials to use for practicing this skill. Ask *where* questions about the locations of objects found in these pictures, and have the student point to them.

When-What Questions
Present common objects from several categories. Ask a *when-what* question, such as "When you are hungry, what do you want?" Help the student choose an item from the food category. Pictures also may be used. Present three catalog pictures—a swim suit, a pair of gloves, and underwear. Then ask, "When you go outside, what do you wear on your hands?"

When Questions

Understanding time is a difficult task. Begin this exercise by choosing several times of day that your student recognizes or relates to, such as getting up in the morning, eating lunch at noon, and going to bed at night. Ask simple *when* questions, such as "When do you sleep?" and "When do you eat lunch?" Present pictures that illustrate these times, and help your student choose the appropriate one. During the day, point out the time as it relates to the routine (for example, "It's morning. We eat breakfast in the morning" or "It's dark. We go to bed at night when it's dark." As the student becomes familiar with general time terms, you may be able to add the concepts of days, months, years, and specific times using a simplified clock.

Why Questions

Reasoning is required for a youngster to learn to answer *why* questions. Present a choice of three situation pictures, such as a person with dirty hands, another person falling, and a third person laughing. Ask "Why do we get washed?" Help your student choose the picture that depicts the right answer.

How Questions

Play-acting can be a fun way to teach your youngster to respond to *how* questions. Ask a simple *how* question, such as "How do you drink milk?" Help the student act out the correct gesture. At a more difficult level, use action sequence pictures or photos that show the basic steps to complete a task. For example, show your youngster a sequence of three photos of a girl putting toothpaste on a toothbrush, brushing her teeth, and rinsing her mouth. Mix up the pictures, and have your student place them in the proper order when you ask, "How do you brush your teeth?"

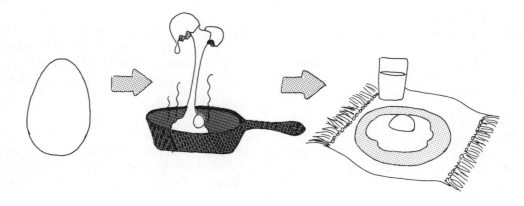

If-What and *What-If* Questions

If-what and *what-if* questions required reasoning. Give the student a condition, such as "If you fall, . . ." Then ask, "What will happen?" Present a choice of three pictures, and have the student point to the one that depicts the appropriate outcome.

Varied Questions

Once the student learns to answer questions from specific individual categories, such as *what* and *who* questions, you can mix up the order of the questions. For example, show a picture of a boy eating an ice-cream cone at the park. Ask "Who is eating ice cream?" and help your student point to the boy. Then ask, "Where is the boy?" and help your student point to the park. Finally, ask "What is the boy eating?" and help the student find the ice-cream cone. If the student has difficulty finding the correct answer, say "When I ask a *who* question, you must answer with a person," or "When I ask a *where* question, you must find a place." At home, have your student point to people, places, and things when you ask these kinds of questions.

Teach your student to respond to questions by using gestures or by pointing to pictures or objects in the environment. After gaining the ability to respond easily by pointing or gesturing, the student can begin to answer by using an expressive communication system—talking, signing, picture board, or computerized communication device.

These skills are very difficult for our youngsters, but they are essential to their development. Be sure to give a lot of praise, and make these activities fun.

The Speech Staff

UNDERSTANDING PRONOUNS

Students must recognize others and be able to tell the difference between male and female figures in order to recognize pronouns. For some pronouns, they also must recognize the number concepts of one and more than one. The following activities are designed to teach the basic pronouns *my/mine* and *your/yours*, *he/she/they*, and *his/hers/theirs*.

My/Mine and Your/Yours
These concepts are very difficult for our students to grasp because "my" to the youngster will mean his or her own object. For example, when you ask a youngster to "Show me *my* shirt," you are referring to your own shirt. However, to the youngster, "my" is something that belongs to him or her. To help your student understand, point to yourself as you say "Show me *my* shirt." Then, when giving the directive, "Show me *your* shirt," point to the student. Practice this skill using clothing, body parts, and possessions.

He, She, and They
Begin to teach these pronouns by saying, "A man is called *he*, a woman is called *she*, and more than one person is called *they*." Present three pictures, one showing a man, a second picture showing a woman, and a third picture showing several people. All of these people must have one thing in common, such as they are all wearing pants. Ask your student to "Find the picture where *she* is wearing pants." You may have to remind the student that "A woman is called *she*." Continue to give clues until your student recognizes the pronouns *he, she,* and *they* and associates them with the correct people. Use these pronouns when talking about real people who are carrying out actions. Photos also may be used to practice this skill.

His, Hers, and Theirs
Possessions that belong to others are referred to as *his, hers,* and *theirs*. Tell your student, "Something that belongs to a boy is *his,* and something a girl has is *hers*. When more than one person owns something, it is *theirs*." Use the same picture or photo sets as were used in teaching *he, she,* and *they*. Present a set of three pictures, and ask your student to "Find *his* pants." If necessary, remind the student that "Something that belongs to a boy is *his*." Practice this skill until the student no longer needs the clue to recognize objects that are *his, hers,* or *theirs*.

Use these pronouns throughout the day to point out family members' possessions and to describe the actions of those around you: "Sally is taking *her* plate to the sink. Now she is washing *her* dishes. I am taking *my* plate to the sink. Bring *your* plate here." Soon the student will be able to understand these pronoun concepts as they relate to real situations.

The Speech Staff

RECOGNIZING VERB TENSE: PRESENT, PAST, AND FUTURE

When students understand the time concepts of "now" or "today," "yesterday" and "tomorrow," they are ready to begin recognizing verbs or action words as they relate to the present (*now*), the past (*yesterday*), and the future (*tomorrow*). Introduce these concepts by stressing actions words while discussing daily routines. For example, you might say "Today is Saturday. We *go* shopping on Saturday. Yesterday was Friday. We *went* bowling on Friday. Tomorrow will be Sunday. We *will go* to church." This helps your student to hear the differences in action words while learning about time and daily routines. You may use pictures to depict these various activities, and ask the student to point to the appropriate picture when you ask "Where will we go tomorrow?"

Present a sequence of three pictures or photos showing a person who is going to do an action, a person doing that action, and a person who has finished that same action. One picture could show a girl gathering ingredients to bake cookies, the second picture would show her making the cookies, and the third picture would show the baked cookies. Mix up the pictures, and then have the student place them in the proper order. Ask the student to show you "The girl is going to bake cookies." Then say "Find the picture where the girl is baking cookies right now." Finally, ask your youngster to find the picture where "The girl is finished. She baked the cookies." As the student becomes more skilled, ask for the pictures in varied order and omit the clue words "now" and "finished."

Children's cookbooks and other "how to" books often include pictures of the basic steps of carrying out familiar chores. These are excellent materials for teaching recognition of the present, past, and future tense of verbs. Photo sequences of your student and other family members carrying out routine tasks also are excellent materials . They also can be used to teach the basic steps of routine tasks, and they can help the student learn to carry out those tasks more independently.

Enjoy these activities with your student. You'll be surprised just how valuable these time concepts are! Among other benefits, they will help your student wait for holidays and anticipated events more patiently.

The Speech Staff

Expressive Language

COMMUNICATING WANTS AND NEEDS

Those who cannot talk, sign, or use some formal system of alternate communication to express their wants and needs often show their frustration by disruptive and inappropriate behavior. It is important to establish a simple expressive communication system to help them indicate their wants and needs.

Once students are able to communicate by pointing to items, a formal system of expression must be developed, using either speech, sign language, picture boards, or another formal system of alternate communication. The Individual Educational Planning Committee should establish each student's communication system. It is absolutely essential to use the same system consistently at home and at school.

To help your student practice communicating wants and needs, present a choice of three items, such as three types of beverages for breakfast. Help the student point to the chosen item and then use the expressive system to "say" what the item is.

Eventually the student should learn to indicate wants and needs for objects that are not present. This requires two skills: memory and object permanence—the knowledge that an object exists even when it is out of sight. As the ability to ask for present or absent objects increases, and as the student becomes more able to express wants and needs, the less frustrated and better behaved the student will be.

Sometimes you will have to say "no" to a request. Praise the student for making the request ("I'm glad you asked me for a cookie"), and redirect the student's interest to another area ("but we are going to eat dinner now"). You may want to set up a "contingency" ("If you eat a good dinner then you may have a cookie"). In the case of a tantrum, remove the student from the area until behavior is acceptable again. By using redirection and consistent behavior management, you will help your student learn to handle these situations.

Try to keep interactions positive and make communication a pleasant and rewarding experience for your student.

The Speech Staff

NAMING AND REQUESTING OBJECTS AND PICTURES

Students who are beginning to talk should be encouraged to make verbal attempts to name or request objects. For those who do not yet speak or attempt to speak, sign language, picture boards, or other alternate communication systems may be used to carry out naming and requesting activities. The student should use the method or methods of expression established in the Individual Educational Plan. Consistency between the home and school in the method of expression is essential if the student is to make the best possible progress.

Choose several objects your student recognizes. Hold the objects up one at a time, and ask "What is this?" A doll or puppet may be used to ask what an item is, and the student may use a doll or puppet to give the answer.

"Grab bag" is fun! Several items are placed in a bag or container. The student reaches in, pulls out one object at a time, and names it. A shopping bag can be used to hold food items, and a laundry basket can hold clothing.

Playing "store" is another fun way for students to request objects. Be the clerk, and help your student request items from you. You may want to include the concept of paying money or tokens to buy objects.

Take turns pointing to items in a room and naming them. Turn the exercise into a game by having the student name items for you to find.

Naming pictures or requesting pictures of items can be practiced in many ways. Look through books and catalogs and have the student name the items you see. Cut out food pictures, glue them to paper plates, and pretend you are ordering and eating food at a restaurant. Make picture books or posters, and practice naming the objects you have included.

Another fun activity involves making a posterboard house. Staple or glue flannel or Velcro pieces onto the windows, doors, and rooms. Then cut out pictures of common items, glue them on index cards, and glue or staple pieces of Velcro or flannel on the back. You and your student can take turns requesting the pictured objects, taking the picture cards off the house, and putting them back on.

Use your imagination to make up games and use materials in new ways! Select relevant vocabulary for the activities. Remember to expect eye contact, attending, and compliance—the learning basics. Allow enough time for your student to respond, and give praise for all attempts at expressing names or requesting objects.

The Speech Staff

NAMING FUNCTIONS OF OBJECTS AND PICTURES

Once students are able to name or request objects, they begin to learn the action words that describe the object's function. First they learn to understand the action words when directed to "Find the one we (action) with." Then they begin to name the actions associated with specific objects.

To help your student acquire this skill, present common objects that the youngster recognizes. Have the student name the objects, and then ask "What do you do with (object)?" At first, you may need to give a clue. Review the activity on the receptive (comprehending) level by placing three objects on the table, saying "Find the one we (action) with." Then hold up each object, and ask "What do you do with (object)?" If the student still experiences difficulty, present a choice of three answers. If the student chooses the wrong action, demonstrate that incorrect action, tell the student that the answer was wrong, and then act out the correct action as a further clue. Students usually enjoy the silliness of adults using objects incorrectly, and often they come up with the correct answer after receiving the clue. As the student becomes more skilled with this activity, decrease the clues. Practice the activity often throughout the day so the student learns to tell the functions of common objects used at home and at school.

Naming functions of pictured objects is the next skill your student will practice. Present a picture of an object, and ask "What do you do with (object)?" Once the student has mastered the basic task, you can practice categorization skills by sorting the pictures into piles of items that have the same functions.

These activities will help your student express actions associated with familiar objects. Action words, when combined with object names, often are a student's first two-word phrases. This basic task will help lay the foundation for expressive sentence building, a skill which will greatly enhance your student's communication abilities.

The Speech Staff

NAMING AND REQUESTING ACTIONS (VERBS)

Expressing action words, or verbs, is one of the basic language skills that students must learn. It is necessary for making requests and describing events, and it is an essential part of sentence building.

The student must be able to recognize and respond to requests for actions or pictured actions on the receptive (understanding) level. Once that is accomplished, the student is ready to begin expressing verbs.

Help your student by performing simple actions or pantomimes—running, eating, sleeping, or jumping—while asking "What am I doing?" The student should answer with at least a single action word, using an expressive communication system. Point to others in the environment, and ask your student to tell what the person or animal is doing.

Students enjoy giving one-word action commands that must be followed, as in the game "Simon Says." Silly actions, such as "snoring" for sleep, often become favorite requests. (The youngsters delight in seeing adults act silly!) This type of playful interaction greatly enhances enjoyment of the activity and communication in general!

Toys are excellent for stimulating students to express actions. Dolls or puppets can be used to perform actions for the student to describe or request. Mechanical toys also are great sources of action that youngsters love! A large variety of inexpensive and highly motivating wind-up and battery-operated toys are available. Bubbles, balls, and cars also stimulate action requests. Your student may request "blow" for bubbles, "roll" or "throw" for the ball, and "push" for the car.

Use photographs of your student and other family members, friends, and pets carrying out simple actions. Make action books or collages using action pictures cut from magazines. Coloring books and children's storybooks also illustrate many simple actions. As you read the story, ask your student to describe each picture, using the correct action words.

Let your imagination go, and discover how many enjoyable activities you can share while helping your student learn to express actions!

The Speech Staff

EXPRESSING LOCATIONS AND PREPOSITIONS

Locations of objects are indicated in a general way by noun places and in a specific way by prepositions that tell the relationship between two objects. For example, in the sentence "The soap is in the dish," the noun location is *dish*, and *in* is the preposition that tells the relationship between soap and dish. When students are able to recognize noun locations and prepositions, they are ready to begin learning to express these terms.

First they learn to express noun locations when asked simple *Where* questions. A typical response to the question "Where's the car?" would be "Floor." When students can name those simple locations consistently, they begin to practice expressing prepositions. Usually, prepositions are learned in pairs, beginning with the simplest terms—*in/out, on/off, up/down,* and *over/under.*

Later, students learn more complex prepositions, such as *in front of/in back of* or *behind, beside* or *next to, between, through,* and *around.* Teach these in pairs also; and whenever possible, use real objects to demonstrate the locations.

Begin practice by placing a book on the table, and asking "Where's the book?" Help your student express "*On* the table" and then "*Off* the table." Play hiding games to teach locations and prepositions. While the student's eyes are closed, hide a shoe or other familiar object under your chair. (Be sure to put the objects fairly close to the student at first, so they are easy to find. As the student gets better at looking for the objects, you can hide them in less obvious places.) Ask "Where's the shoe?" Help the student find the object and tell you where it was hidden, using the phrase "Under (the) chair." For fun, put objects in silly places, such as putting the shoe on your head. Ask "Where's the shoe?" and help the student tell you "Shoe (on) head." Then ask "Do we wear a shoe on our head?" Help the student answer "No, (on) foot."

Practice expressing noun locations and prepositions during daily chores such as setting the table, doing laundry, or cleaning. Ask "Where is the napkin?" and "Where do we put the dirty clothes?" and "Where do we keep the vacuum?" Help your student express the correct prepositions and noun locations: "Under (the) fork" and "In (the) washer" and "In (the) closet."

You may also use pictures to practice these terms. Almost any picture containing two or more objects can be used to practice expression of prepositions and noun locations. Look for storybook and magazine pictures that depict objects and people in various positions. Use photos of family members carrying out simple actions. Present a simple picture, such as a boy holding a glass of milk, and ask "Where's the milk?" Help your youngster tell "The milk is *in* the *glass*" and "The glass is *on* the *table*" and "The boy is *in* the *kitchen.*"

These are difficult but important concepts for students to learn. Help your student feel successful while working on these skills, and give frequent praise for hard work.

The Speech Staff

EXPRESSING TWO-WORD AND THREE-WORD PHRASES

Once students can name and request objects as well as actions, using one word at a time, they may begin to combine those words to make phrases. One way to stimulate this skill is to use toys. First, have your student name or request an object; for example, a ball. Ask "What do you want me to do with the ball?" If the student has difficulty remembering actions associated with that object, offer some choices: "Do you want me to throw it, roll it, or kick it?" You may want to act out each action as you say it, to help strengthen the student's understanding of the action verbs.

When students can name or request the object and the action in sequence, they will begin to combine the action word with the object name. "Baby sleep," "roll ball," and "blow bubbles" are typical two-word phrases used by youngsters when they are playing with a doll, a ball, and bubbles.

As they become more skilled at using two-word phrases, you can expect them to add a third part to the phrase. For example, ask "Who do you want me to roll the ball to?" If the student answers "Roll ball," you might say "Roll (the) ball (to) me" to stimulate the three-word phrase. After the student says "Push car," ask "Where do you want me to push the car?" Encourage the student to respond in the three-word phrase, "Push (the) car (on the) floor." Pictures also can be used to stimulate the student to use two-word and three-word phrases.

Throughout the day, use names of people and objects, common actions, and place locations to stimulate your student to use two- and three-word phrases. First, however, make sure your student can use the individual words before you expect them to be combined into phrases. Make communication a positive and pleasant activity. Give encouragement and frequent praise, and see how quickly your student learns to use phrases!

The Speech Staff

REQUESTING "MORE"

Once students learn to communicate for something they want or need, they should learn appropriate ways to ask for "more." They may grab at an item, look at the item then look at you, use your hand as a tool to get another item, or point to the item repeatedly. Students who talk may say the item name, and those who use an alternate communication system may repeat the item name by sign, picture board, or computerized voice device. Initially, many of these means of requesting "more" are acceptable, but eventually you will want your student to either say, sign, use a picture board, or use a computerized voice device to indicate "more." Nonverbal students often are taught to use either the sign "more" or a picture of the sign along with the computerized voice device. The sign is made by touching the index finger and thumb together on both hands, then tapping the fingertips of both hands together twice. You might choose a picture that depicts a person holding one item and receiving a second one. Use whatever best represents "more" to your student.

Help your student use "more" with a request for a second item, such as "more cookie." This may be your youngster's first two-word phrase!

The Speech Staff

EXPRESSING ADJECTIVES: SIZE, COLOR, AND NUMBER

Adjectives are words used to provide descriptions. Once students understand the basic adjectives of size, color, and number, they can be expected to express these concepts.

There are many opportunities to use adjectives throughout the day, using objects that are necessary to carry out daily living chores.

Size

Requesting *big* and *little* food items is a highly motivating activity. When offering food, allow your student to choose either a little or big portion and tell others whether they can take big or little portions. In the kitchen, expect the student to request big or little spoons, cups, bowls, and other items. In daily living activities, such as cleaning, require the student to talk about big and little buckets, sponges, towels, and other equipment items. Once the student can express *big* and *little* using real objects, introduce pictures of items that vary in size. Help your student to express these differences, using the terms *big* and *little*.

Color

Requesting objects of specific colors is a skill that can be integrated into almost any activity. For example, when your student asks for a piece of candy, present a choice of two different colors; and require your youngster to request specific colors of clothing when dressing each morning.

Use color unit books to find pictures of items that are a specific color. Have the student name the items, using a two-word phrase describing the color ("blue car").

Teach color activities throughout the day in casual situations. Make the learning situation relevant to the student's needs.

Number

Learning to express numbers when requesting objects is an important skill for functioning independently. When preparing food, setting the table, or passing out items necessary to complete a task, ask "How many (objects) do you need?" Require the student to ask for a specific amount when requesting a treat: "Two cookies." If necessary, help the student count the number of items, and then ask "How many?" Begin with requests for one to five items, and gradually increase the number.

Present pictures of various items, and ask "How many?" Help the student count the items first, if necessary.

Throughout the day, require the student to tell "how many" or request a specific number of items whenever possible. Vary the activities often, and carry them out in natural situations. Be sure to acknowledge all attempts, and praise the student for a job well done!

The Speech Staff

EXPRESSING OPPOSITE ADJECTIVES

Adjectives are terms that are used to describe people, places, and things. Usually they are taught in pairs. When students are able to recognize and discriminate between objects, people, or places when adjectives have been used to describe them, they are ready to begin expressing these terms.

There are many opportunities for teaching opposite terms while carrying out daily routines. When your student requests something, give a choice of two objects; or give the wrong object, such as a small cookie rather than a large one, and see if the student will correct you by using the appropriate opposite word. Your student will enjoy the fun of this playful situation while learning to express opposite adjectives!

Hot/Cold

At mealtime, give your student the option of having hot or cold food. For example, you might offer a choice between hot or cold chocolate milk. Show the difference between the two, and help your student express the correct descriptive term when making requests.

Big/Little

When offering food, encourage the student to ask for a big or a little portion. When folding laundry, have the student sort towels or socks, and ask which items are big or little. Throughout the day, help your student express these terms to describe sizes.

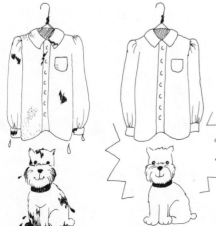

Clean/Dirty

Before washing dishes, clothes, or hands, ask if the plates, laundry items, or hands are clean or dirty. After they are washed, ask the student to describe them, using the term *clean*. Help the student express clean and dirty often while carrying out daily chores.

Wet/Dry
These terms usually can be expressed during the same activities as those used for clean and dirty.

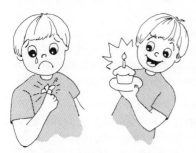

Happy/Sad
Ask the student "How are you feeling?" If the student is not able to answer spontaneously, describe how the youngster looks, saying "You're smiling. Do you feel happy or sad?" Help your student express the correct emotion word. Ask how others feel, and have the student describe their emotions.

Pictures and photographs are good materials for teaching these opposite emotion words. Present a picture, and say "This lady is crying. How do you think she feels?" You may need to ask "Is she happy or sad?" Then present an opposite picture depicting *happy,* and have the student use a phrase or sentence that describes the emotion.

Empty/Full
Before serving food, ask "Is your plate empty or full?" After the student answers correctly, serve the food and ask the question again. Help the student use the terms *empty* and *full* in relevant situations while eating, cooking, cleaning, emptying wastebaskets, and doing other household chores.

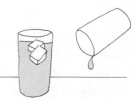

Hard/Soft and Rough/Smooth
Choose some common objects that are hard or soft, rough or smooth. Have the student touch or handle the objects and describe how they feel. Once the student can do this, hide the objects in a bag. Have the student feel the objects one at a time and describe how each feels. Then see if the student can identify the object by touch alone.

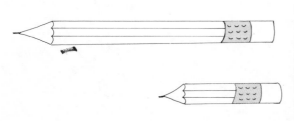

Long/Short and Tall/Short
Offer long and short carrot sticks, bread sticks, or pretzels. Have the student ask for them, using the terms *long* and *short.* Use pencils, pants, coats, and other objects to stimulate the student to use these adjectives. To teach the terms *tall* and *short,* compare the height of family members. Encourage the student to express these terms in appropriate situations throughout the day.

The Speech Staff

EXPRESSING NONEXISTENCE

It is important for students to be able to indicate when something is not present, or "nonexistent." The ability to express nonexistence is a frequent requirement for workshops and skill centers. For example, while working at a task such as assembling nuts and bolts, students need to be able to express when they run out of a specific item.

To practice this skill, place some common objects on the table. Say "Give me (object that is present)." After several requests, ask for an object that is not on the table. Silly things—a dog, a snowball, or a pizza—often bring immediate responses. The youngsters may giggle and give curious looks. Help your student look at all the objects on the table and decide that the object you requested is not present. Then say "There's no (object)," and help your student learn to express this phrase.

Another fun activity involves the use of the phrase "all gone." Place several bowls upside-down on the table. Put a few pieces of food under some of the bowls. Slide the bowls around, and then ask the student to "Choose the bowls where you think the food is hidden." When there is no food present, help your student say "There's no food" or "Food's all gone!"

Incorporate the concept of nonexistence, using the phrases "There's no (object)" and "(object's) all gone" into relevant situations throughout the day.

Let us know of enjoyable activities you have used that teach this skill, so we can share them with other parents.

The Speech Staff

EXPRESSING "YES" AND "NO," "IS" AND "IS NOT"

Yes and No

Being able to express "yes" and "no" is a skill that is helpful in many situations. For example, youngsters who are unable to express themselves well can respond to questions by saying "yes" and "no."

Practice this skill by frequently asking your student questions about familiar objects and routines. Offer edible and nonedible objects, and ask "Do you want to eat this?" Help your youngster express either "yes" or "no" appropriately. The student may respond by saying, signing, using a symbol or picture board, using a communication device, or by shaking or nodding the head.

Show your student a spoon, and ask a silly question: "Is this a dog?" Youngsters delight in correcting an adult: "No! It's a spoon." In learning to correct the error by expressing "no," the student also learns how to repair a breakdown in communication. This skill can be useful in many daily situations.

Is and Is Not

Present a cup or a picture of a cup, and ask a silly question: "Is this a pan?" Help the student express "No, it's not a pan. It's a cup." Then ask the correct question, "Is this a cup?" and help the student say "Yes, it is." To help the student learn to correct errors or breakdowns in communication, present a sock, and say "This is a hat." Assist the student in correcting your error by saying, "No, it's not! It's a sock."

Throughout the day, ask routine questions that require *yes* or *no, is* or *is not/(isn't)* responses. As this skill improves, the student will be able to convey more information. This will help lessen frustration caused by the communication disorder.

The Speech Staff

EXPRESSING PLURALS

When naming or requesting more than one of a specific object, we use a plural form of the item, usually by adding an *s* or *es.* For example, *spoons* and *glasses* are the regular plural forms of the nouns *spoon* and *glass.*

To practice this language skill, present an object and have the student name it. Then present another of the same object, and say "Now you have two _____." Let the student provide the correct regular form by adding an *s* or *es* to the object name.

Play "store," and have the student practice buying sets of items, using the plural forms. At snacktime or mealtime, help the student request one or more of a food item. Using the numbers *one* and *two* to indicate the difference when asking for a cookie or cookies is highly motivating. Stressing the *s* as you say the plural noun may help your student to remember and include it when making a request. Pairs of objects in pictures also may be used to label and practice regular plural forms of nouns.

Irregular plurals are formed when a word must have the spelling changed for requests of more than one item. For example, mouse, knife and foot all require changes in spelling when pluralized, becoming mice, knives, and feet. These are learned basically through drill and use. Use picture cards to practice these irregular plurals: "Here is one foot. Here are two _____."

Use these regular and irregular plural forms throughout the day whenever appropriate. You'll be surprised at how many opportunities there are to use the plural form of nouns in your daily routine.

The Speech Staff

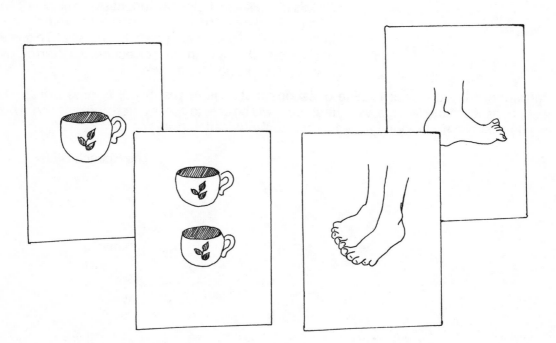

EXPRESSING CATEGORIZATION

Categorization, or grouping items by similarities, requires a high level of thought and mental organization. Once students can sort items by category, they can practice expressive categorization skills.

Request your student to "Tell me the name of a food." If the student has difficulty remembering the name of a food item, you may need to tell the function of the category: "A food is something we eat." Then repeat the direction: "Now can you tell me the name of a food, or something that we eat?" It may be necessary also to present picture cards or objects from several categories, let the student find the ones within the requested category, then have the student name the items. Your goal is to eventually ask the question and have the student answer spontaneously.

When the student is able to name items within a category, present several objects or pictures from the same category. Direct the student to name the category: "Look at all these ojects or pictures and tell me what they are called." At first, you may need to name all the items and then give their function: "This is a cookie, some chips, and an apple. All these are things we eat. What do we call things we eat?" With practice, the student should be able to name foods, toys, clothes, furniture, people, animals, and other basic categories.

Youngsters often enjoy using objects to carry out categorization tasks. Empty food containers, doll clothing and dollhouse furniture, and cake decorating miniatures are appealing objects that may help keep the student's attention.

You may want to make category books or picture collages. Catalogs are a quick resource, where many pictures from a category are shown on the same page or section.

Share some fun categorization activities and watch your student increase the ability to communicate these complex language concepts!

The Speech Staff

NAMING AND REQUESTING OBJECTS
NEEDED FOR ROUTINE TASKS

Being able to name or request objects that are needed to carry out routine tasks helps students become more self-sufficient. They must be able to remember and name the items needed for a task before they can be able to sequence the steps to do that task. It also helps them be able to request these objects, especially when they are missing.

There are many ways to practice this skill. Say to the student, "Let's make some pudding." Talk about all the things needed to make pudding. If the student has difficulty remembering them, prepare picture cards that show the necessary items. As the student names the items, assemble them on the kitchen counter. Omit a few; and then, as you both are making the pudding, ask "What do we need now?" or "What is missing?" As skills improve, provide opportunities for the student to request the needed items without your giving a clue. Allow the student to get the items from drawers, cupboards, and refrigerator.

It may help to cut out pictures of needed objects, paste them on cards, place the cards on a metal ring, and instruct the student to turn to the next picture once the needed item is named and assembled. Gradually eliminate the picture cards, and encourage your student to rely on memory to name the needed items.

Choose cooking, self-care, cleaning, and other activities that will help the student become more independent. You may need to establish rules and times when your student is allowed to carry out these activities independently.

As the ability to name or request needed items improves, the student will become more familiar with the sequence of steps necessary to complete tasks. This will improve the student's ability to carry out familiar chores with less supervision.

The Speech Staff

ANSWERING WH QUESTIONS

Before they are able to answer questions, students must understand what questions are, and must realize that different questions require different kinds of answers. For example, *what* questions require the answer to be an object or action, *who* questions are answered with people's names, and *where* questions are correctly answered with a location. Once students are able to choose the correct picture or object in response to a question, they can be expected to express a word, phrase, or sentence as a response, verbally or through an alternate communication system.

The following are some examples of various question forms and activities that will help your student learn how to answer questions. You may need to use picture or object clues at first, but eventually the student should be able to answer with no clues.

What Questions
Hide an object in a bag. Have the student feel the object but not look at it. Ask "What is it?" Help the student identify the object. At a more complicated level, ask "What do we use to brush our teeth with?" or "What do we do with a toothbrush?" Help the student answer the first question with the object, "Toothbrush," and the second question with the action, "Brush my teeth."

Who Questions
Ask *who* questions about familiar people in the environment. Once the student is able to answer these questions, ask questions about community helpers, such as "Who cuts your hair?" Make sure the questions are about community workers your student recognizes. Help the student respond at the highest possible level of expression.

Where Questions
Ask *where* questions about the location of familiar objects, such as "Where's the refrigerator?" When the student is able to name the place consistently, encourage use of a preposition as well. *In, on, under, beside, in front of, in back of,* and *between* are prepositions the student should learn to use.

When-What Questions
When-What questions require the student to exercise reasoning skills. Establish a condition, such as "When you are thirsty, . . ." Then ask the question, "What do you do?" Help the student understand the condition and then the question. If necessary, use picture clues or simplify the way the question is worded. Practice this skill until the student can answer *when-what* questions without clues.

When Questions

When questions require an understanding of time concepts. Ask simple *when* questions about routine activities, such as "When do you sleep?" or "When do you eat breakfast?" Help your student identify the appropriate times of these events. You may need to use picture clues at first. Review these questions often so the youngster can learn the basic times as related to daily events.

Ask *when* questions about simple actions or situations, such as "When do you sing 'Happy Birthday'?" or "When do you go swimming?" These questions are more difficult than those about daily routines, and again you may have to give clues.

Students who are able to recognize the basic concepts of time, such as days, months, years, and even hours and minutes, may be able to answer *when* questions that require specific times. Help your student to use the highest possible level of expression in responding.

Why Questions

Throughout the day, ask simple *why* questions, such as "Why are you eating breakfast?" or "Why are you washing your hands?" If the student has difficulty, offer some choices: "Is it because you are thirsty, hungry, or dirty?" Practice asking clued *why* questions until the student can answer without clues.

How Questions

Answering *how* questions requires a knowledge of the basic actions and steps necessary to complete a task. For example, "How do you brush your teeth?" involves the steps of getting out the toothbrush and toothpaste, putting toothpaste on the toothbrush, brushing the teeth, and then rinsing the mouth. The student may need to use sequenced picture cards in order to tell those steps. As the student becomes familiar with the steps, fade the use of picture clues. Help the student express phrases and sentences to describe each of the steps necessary for completing the task.

If-What and What-If Questions

Like *why* questions, *if-what* and *what-if* questions require reasoning. Present a condition, such as "If it is raining, . . ." Then continue with the question: "Will you go on a picnic?" Help the student answer the question and explain the reasoning: "No, you'd get wet." If the student has difficulty telling the reason for the answer, give a choice of three reasons, and help the student choose the correct one.

Varied Questions

Once your student can answer specific questions from the individual categories, mix up the order of questions asked. For example, when the student gets up in the morning, ask "When is it?" and "What do you eat in the morning?" and "Where do you eat breakfast?" Finally, ask "Why do you eat breakfast?" You may need to remind the student that *when* questions tell a time, *what* questions are answered with objects or actions, and *where* questions tell places. Ask these varied questions throughout the day in appropriate situations, and help your student learn to distinguish between the question words and the appropriate answer categories.

It is important for your student to learn to answer questions accurately and give the information requested. It will help the student to interact better socially and function more independently. Be sure to recognize all efforts and achievements and give praise often.

The Speech Staff

ASKING QUESTIONS

Many students have difficulty learning to ask simple questions, such as "Can I have (object)?" and "What is this?" or "Who is that?" and "Where is (object)?"

A simple way to begin teaching this skill is to turn the student's requests into questions. When your student makes a request, such as "I want a cookie," say "I know you want a cookie. Let's ask if you can have one. When we ask, we say 'May I have a cookie?'" Throughout the day and with as many people as possible, help your student practice using the question form instead of the "I want" request.

To teach the question form "What is it" or "What is this?" let the student pretend to be the teacher. First, demonstrate the activity by showing a familiar object, and asking "What is this?" Then let the student be the teacher and ask the question, "What is this?" Use familiar objects or pictures of objects, and have the student point to them and ask the question.

Youngsters often enjoy playing "Who Is It?" While the student's eyes are closed, one person leaves the room, then knocks on the closed door. Help the student ask, "Who is it?" and try to guess who is behind the door. You may also show family photos, and let the student ask "Who is it?"

To teach the question, "Where is it?" either you or your student may point to objects in the environment or place objects in a specific location. Help the student ask "Where's the (object)?" Play a hiding game with three bowls placed upside-down on the table. Hide a piece of cookie under one of the bowls, shuffle them around, and help your student ask "Where's the cookie?"

"When" questions are a little more difficult to learn because they involve time concepts. While the student is requesting favorite activities, such as "I want to visit Grandma," ask "Do we visit Grandma on Saturday?" Help the student ask "When do we visit Grandma?" Help the student practice asking questions about routine daily and weekly activities.

Hide several objects in a bag. Help the student ask questions in order to guess the objects. If your student can read, present a number of written questions for the student to ask you. (Questions might include: What is it used for? Is it big or little? What color is it? What shape is it? What is it made from?) The information gained from the clues should lead the student to make a guess, using the question form: "Is it (object)?" Youngsters get really excited when they are able to guess the object correctly. This helps turn a difficult and complicated learning task into a more positive and fun activity.

The Speech Staff

POLITE SOCIAL FORMS

Using greetings and polite social forms, such as "please" and "thank you," will enhance your youngster's social skills and increase positive experiences when communicating with others. Teach your youngster these polite social forms as you encounter appropriate situations. For example, when it is necessary to walk between two people, remind the student to say "Excuse me." Expect the student to say "please" when requesting objects, "thanks" after receiving something, and "you're welcome" after someone has said "thank you." Nonverbal students should use their alternate communication system to express these polite expressions.

Help your youngster ask for things at mealtime by saying "Pass the (item), please." Help the student learn to use silverware properly, take small bites of food, eat slowly, and use a napkin. These social skills, polite requests, and socially appropriate terms will help your student be a more enjoyable person. Require this behavior at home, so the student will learn to act appropriately in all situations. Give praise often, and let your student know you are proud of polite behavior.

The Speech Staff

PERSONAL INFORMATION

Knowing personal information, such as name, address, and phone number, is crucial to our students for a number of reasons. First, knowing and being able to give personal information could save a lot of worry and turmoil if the student should become separated or lost. Second, if there should be an emergency situation involving the police or fire department, a student may need to convey this information. Third, many workshops and skill centers require the student to know this information and carry an identification card.

At time of crisis, a verbal student may be too distressed to remember or convey personal information. Those who are nonverbal or who have unclear speech also must be able to indicate this information. We ask that you have your student carry an identification card at all times, in a wallet or pinned to a piece of clothing. Add pertinent medical information, when appropriate, on the back of the card. Please let us know of any changes in information so we can update your student's card as needed.

It is important for your youngster to practice showing and using the identification card when requested. If the student can talk, the information should be rehearsed verbally; and if the student is using an alternate communication system, the activity should be practiced using that method. Rehearse this task with a number of people in different settings, so your student will be able to respond appropriately in a variety of situations.

The Speech Staff

EXPRESSING PRONOUNS

Learning to express correct pronouns is often a difficult task because of the reversals of terms used when referring to oneself and others. The following activities can be used to teach the basic pronouns *my/mine* and *your/yours; he, she,* and *they;* and *his, hers,* and *theirs.*

My/Mine and Your/Yours

Point to a ball that belongs to your student. Ask "Whose ball is that?" If the student names himself by expressing "That's Tommy's ball," help him use the pronoun *my* or *mine* by saying "That's right. It is Tommy's ball. Tell me, 'It's mine'." Point to items on yourself and to your possessions, and ask "Whose (object) is this?" Help the student express the correct pronoun *your* and *yours* by providing a model to imitate. Practice until your student can use the appropriate pronouns spontaneously.

Youngsters frequently enjoy the element of surprise in an activity such as pulling objects out of a container and asking "Whose (object) is this?" Occasionally give an object to the wrong person while saying "Oh, this toy belongs to Susie." Help your youngster tell you "No! Mine!" or "No! My toy." Offer your own possessions to others, and help your student express "No! Yours!" or "No! Your hat."

No! Yours!

He, She, and They

Although a youngster may recognize people when referred to as *he, she,* or *they,* it is often difficult for them to express these terms. Make sure your youngster recognizes the terms and associates them with the correct people. Once the student can do this, point to people in the environment or in a picture, and ask "What's he doing?" If the student answers "The boy is sitting," give praise, saying "That's right! The boy is sitting. We have another name for a boy. Remember, a boy is called a _____." Help the student use the correct pronoun, and then ask the question again: "What's he doing?"

Take turns playing "Name It." As you are walking outside, or when you are watching TV, point and say "She is a girl. She's driving the car to McDonald's." Then give the student a turn to point to someone and tell what he or she is doing or where they are going.

His, Hers, and Theirs

When referring to the possessions of others, we use the terms *his, hers,* and *theirs.* Hide family members' belongings in a bag, pull out the items one by one, and ask "Whose (object) is this?" Have the student point to the person to whom the object belongs, and help the student say "It's his" (or hers or theirs). Pictures may be used by pointing to objects that appear to belong to specific people, and asking "Whose (object) is that?" You may need to remind the student that something that belongs to a woman is *hers,* something that belongs to a man is *his,* and an object that belongs to two or more people is *theirs.*

During conversations throughout the day, help your youngster use the pronoun forms to describe and name others and refer to their possessions.

The Speech Staff

COMPARING SIZE, QUANTITY, AND QUALITY

Comparisons of size and quantity can be taught easily while you prepare food. Graduated sizes of measuring cups, spoons, bowls, pans, and containers all provide sizes and quantities for the student to compare. As you cook, read the recipe aloud. Whenever possible, present a choice of three different sizes, such as measuring cups—¼ cup, ½ cup, and 1 cup. Ask "Which is ¼ cup? Is it the smallest cup, the middle-sized cup, or the largest cup?" When the student is able to give the information, decrease the use of clues. Throughout the day, encourage the student to use the terms *smallest, biggest,* and *medium* or *middle-sized* when requesting items.

As you shop for groceries, show various sizes of jars, boxes, and cans, and ask "Which one has the most?" and "Which one has the least?" When serving your family, give varied amounts of food and ask "Who has the most food?" and "Who has the least food?" Sometimes you can ask the student to serve the food while you say "Dad gets the most. Baby gets the least. Tim gets more than Jane."

Teach other quantity words, such as *a few, a lot, many, a little, one,* and *some.* Help your student use these terms to request snacks, toys, and other things. But just because the student asks for "Many cookies" doesn't mean you should always give them. Praise the student for asking for the cookies by using such good language, but explain that "You may have just *one* cookie before dinner." Be consistent in allowing the student to have only the amount you would permit normally.

When you are sure the student understands and can express the basic comparisons, you can introduce terms to compare more complex sizes, quantities, and qualities. Some of these include *light/heavy, light/dark, fat/thin, wet/dry, happy/sad, fast/slow,* and *clean/dirty.*

Help your student use these comparison terms to request and describe items. You'll be surprised at the number of daily activities that can include comparisons of size, quantity, and quality. By learning a variety of terms in useful settings within the daily routine, your student will be more likely to use them in other situations. Soon you will hear spontaneous requests for the *biggest* apple, the *shortest* glass, the *longest pencil,* and the *fastest* toy!

The Speech Staff

EXPRESSING VERB TENSE: PRESENT, PAST, AND FUTURE

Expressing various time concepts usually requires the use of different verb tenses. When we talk about something that happened yesterday, we use the past tense ("Yesterday I *went* skating"); and when talking about tomorrow, we use the future tense of the verb ("Tomorrow we *will go* skating"). Engage your student in conversation about things that have happened in the past, things that are happening in the present, and things that will happen in the future. Help your student tell about those activities, using the correct verb tenses. You may want to use a large calendar to help your student understand the concepts.

Take photos of your family doing routine activities. Discuss when these activities occur, and have the student use the proper action words when talking about them. Children's cookbooks and other "how to" books usually offer sequence pictures that can be used to teach basic verb tenses. Show your student a picture of a girl taking out toothbrush and toothpaste, and ask "What is she going to do?" Help your student express the future by saying "She is going to brush her teeth." Then show a picture of the girl brushing, and ask "What is she doing now?" Help the student say "She is brushing her teeth." Finally, show a picture of the girl after brushing, and ask "What did she do?" Again, help the student say "She brushed her teeth." This activity also teaches correct sequences, how to respond to simple *what* and *how* questions, and the basics of daily routines.

Use action toys to teach past, present, and future. Present a truck, and ask "What do you want me to do?" When the student uses the correct verb tense to describe the desired action ("Push the truck to me"), carry out the action, and ask "What did I do?" Help the student use the past tense *pushed* to describe your action.

Include these time concepts often in your daily conversations. Being able to express verbs in the present, past, and future tense will help your student better express information about daily routines. The student also will learn to be more patient in waiting for future activities and events. You'll be amazed at how quickly your student learns to recognize the times and days when enjoyable activities occur!

The Speech Staff

MAKING INTRODUCTIONS

Learning how to introduce people to one another is a social skill that enhances communication and opens the door to simple conversations. Tell your student, "When introducing two people who do not know each other, we say 'Joe, this is Tom' and 'Tom, this is Joe.' We look at both people as we say their names."

Cue cards will help your student practice how to make an introduction. Write the names of friends and family on slips of paper, and help your student make "pretend" introductions. If the student has difficulty reading the names, glue a photo of the person next to the printed name. Continue to practice until the student can make introductions without using the cue cards.

It's great fun to pretend that you and your student are meeting for the first time and are just getting to know one another. This play-acting will help your student develop better social and communication skills, so practice often!

The Speech Staff

CONVERSING

Participating in a conversation is an extremely challenging task for our students. Even when someone else starts a conversation, often it is difficult to *maintain* a conversation—to think of things to say and to remember to remain on the topic being discussed.

Help your youngster plan some short conversations, and discuss the boundaries of subjects that are within that topic area. For example, if you are discussing a favorite TV show, it is appropriate to talk about the show and its characters in general, a specific episode of the show, and even events that occurred while watching the show; but it is *not* appropriate to talk about totally unrelated subjects. Often, when our youngsters introduce unrelated topics, they are subjected to social rejection; and frequently they don't understand what they have done wrong. It is important to give your youngster many opportunities to practice conversing with friends and family. If the student wanders from the topic being discussed, stop the conversation immediately. Remind the student of the topic, and ask "Are you talking about that subject?" This should make the student aware of inappropriate activity *at the time the error occurs.* Help the student return to the topic, and then give praise for sharing an enjoyable conversation.

Once the student can maintain a conversation, you can begin to practice how to *initiate,* or start, a discussion. Tell your student, "After two people have been introduced or when they meet each other, they will want to talk. Some things they might say are "Hi! How are you today? . . . What have you been doing lately? . . . Nice day, isn't it? . . . You look pretty today. . . . How is (friend or family member)? . . . Did you see the (TV show or sporting event)?"

Use these and other conversation starters, and help your student practice with friends and family. You might plan conversations for when Mom or Dad comes home from work or when friends are visiting. Write some of the topic ideas in case the student is stumped for something to say and wants to check the list for ideas.

It is important for the student to understand that it is not appropriate to initiate conversations with strangers. Review some of the people with whom the student can safely initiate conversations, and stress that it is not acceptable to talk to strangers.

A third conversational skill is *repairing* conversations when a breakdown or misunderstanding occurs. This skill can be practiced by intentionally misunderstanding something your student has said or by giving some information that the student will recognize as wrong. Help your student recognize the "error" and correct the situation. For example, on a snowy day, you might say "It certainly is warm today. I think I'll put on my swimsuit and go outside." As the student understands the task, the errors should be more and more subtle, until the student is easily able to repair minor breakdowns in conversations.

The Speech Staff

SEQUENCING EVENTS

It is important for our students to learn the basic sequence of events needed to complete routine tasks; to be able to visually sequence pictures that show those basic steps; and to express those steps verbally or through an alternate communication system.

Take sequenced photos of your student and other family members carrying out routine chores. Have the student arrange the photos in the order in which the events occur. Practice sequence tasks by showing step-by-step illustrations contained in instruction manuals, children's cookbooks, and "how-to" articles and books. At first, present no more than three pictures. Gradually increase the number until the student can sequence six to eight pictures. Help the student use the highest possible level of expression to tell what is happening in each picture. For example, your student describes a picture of a boy getting his toothbrush and toothpaste: "Tom get toothbrush." Respond by saying "Yes, Tom is getting his toothbrush and toothpaste. He is going to brush his teeth before he goes to bed." In this way, you are expanding on sentence length and complexity while increasing the ideas that are presented.

Use picture sequence sets to help the student carry out routine chores more independently. Place a sequenced set of pictures on a metal ring. Have the student express the action pictured, carry out the action, turn to the next picture, and again express and carry out the action. Make sure the action sequence pictures are relevant to the student's daily routine. By using these flip-card picture sequences, your student can practice and improve self-management skills.

Praise your student's increased independence and ability to talk about activities and events. It is important for our students to feel that their efforts are being recognized and that what they are learning is worthwhile. Most important of all, it is essential that they feel loved and accepted while they are striving to learn new tasks!

The Speech Staff

Index of Skills

INDEX OF SKILLS

The following list of skills is from the Communication Skills Inventories described in *Evaluating Acquired Skills in Communication (EASIC)*. The numbers in bold print following each skill refer to page numbers in the *After School Communication Activity Book*.

Pre-Language

Sensory Stimulation
1. Responding to environmental sound, **8**
2. Responding to the human voice, **8**
3. Establishing and following a line of visual regard, **9**
4. Responding to visual stimulation (focusing and tracking), **9, 10**
5. Returning, maintaining, and establishing appropriate eye contact, **7**
6. Responding to visual stimulation (regard, reaching, and grasping), **9**

Object Relations
7. Comprehending object permanence, **11**
8. Comprehending the function of common objects, **12, 13**

Means-Ends Causality
9. Using an object as a tool to attain a desired item, **14-15**
10. Acquiring adult attention, **16**
11. Using an adult to attain a desired object or action, **25**
12. Manipulating an object or toy to achieve a desired outcome, **12**

Motor Imitation
13. Imitating motor acts involving the use of objects, **17**
14. Imitating motor acts involving the use of body parts, **17**

Matching
15. Matching identical objects, **18**

Rejection, Negation, and Affirmation
16. Rejecting and affirming objects, **20, 77**
17. Understanding negation (inhibiting action in response to "No"), **21**

Comprehension and Use of Communicative Gestures
18. Using nonverbal greetings, **22**
19. Responding to a verbal command with gestures, **23-24**
20. Responding to a command with gestures involving an object, **31-32**
21. Indicating choices, **25**
22. Communicating basic wants and needs nonverbally, **25, 65**
23. Expressing desire for recurrence of object or action nonverbally, **71**

Social Interaction
24. Maintaining and establishing appropriate physical proximity, **7**
25. Turn-taking, **7**
26. Appropriate and symbolic play, **26, 27-28**

Receptive Language I

Noun Labels and Object Identification
1. Identifying common objects by noun labels, **31-32**
2. Identifying familiar people by noun agents, **31-32**
3. Identifying body parts by noun labels, **31-32**

Commands
4. Responding to simple directional commands involving objects, **23-24**
5. Responding to commands involving body parts, **23-24**
6. Responding to commands involving two objects, **23-24**

Expressive Language II

Labels: Nouns and Pronouns
1. Expressing noun labels for objects and people in pictures, **66**
2. Expressing noun labels for objects needed for routine tasks, **66, 80**
3. Expressing personal pronouns *he, she, they*, **87**
4. Expressing possessive pronouns *my/mine, your/yours*, **87**
5. Expressing possessive pronouns *his, hers, theirs*, **88**

Verbs
6. Expressing the function of objects, **67**
7. Expressing verbs in pictures, **68**
8. Expressing a verb in response to a *what-when* question, **68, 81-83**
9. Expressing present, past, and future tense of verbs, **90**

Affirmation and Negation
10. Expressing affirmation and negation of an object, **20, 77**

Locations and Prepositions
11. Expressing locations and prepositions involving objects, **69**
12. Expressing locations and prepositions involving objects in pictures, **69**

Plurals
13. Expressing plurals, **78**

Categorization
14. Expressing noun labels for categories in pictures, **79**

Adjectives and Attributes
15. Expressing quality adjectives and attributes in pictures, **72-73, 74-75**
16. Expressing comparatives and superlatives, **74-75, 89**

Three-Word Phrases
17. Expressing three-word phrases involving pictures, **70**

Interrogatives
18. Expressing a noun agent in response to a *who* question, **81-83**
19. Expressing a noun in response to a *when-what* question, **81-83**
20. Expressing a noun location in response to a *where* question, **81-83**
21. Answering *when* questions, **81-83**
22. Answering *how* questions, **81-83**
23. Answering *why* questions, **81-83**
24. Answering *what-if* questions, **81-83**
25. Answering *if-what* questions, **81-83**
26. Answering varied questions, **81-83**
27. Asking questions, **84**

Social Interaction
28. Communicative turn-taking, **7**
29. Maintaining a topic, initiating conversation, repairing communication, **77, 91, 92-93**

Sequencing and Sentence Structure
30. Using connected language to describe a picture sequence story, **92-93, 94**
31. Connected language analysis (spontaneous and elicited utterances), **92-93**